Critical Narrative Analysis in Psy

Also by Stephen Frosh

AFTER WORDS: The Personal in Gender, Culture and Psychotherapy

IDENTITY CRISIS: Modernity, Psychoanalysis and the Self

FOR AND AGAINST PSYCHOANALYSIS

KEY CONCEPTS IN PSYCHOANALYSIS

THE POLITICS OF PSYCHOANALYSIS: An Introduction to Freudian
and Post-Freudian Theory

PSYCHOANALYSIS AND PSYCHOLOGY: Minding the Gap

SEXUAL DIFFERENCE: Masculinity and Psychoanalysis

CHILD SEXUAL ABUSE (*with D. Glaser*)

YOUNG MASCULINITIES: Understanding Boys in Contemporary Society
(*with A. Phoenix and R. Pattman*)

HATE AND THE JEWISH SCIENCE: Anti-Semitism, Nazism and
Psychoanalysis

Critical Narrative Analysis in Psychology

A Guide to Practice

Revised Edition

Peter Emerson

and

Stephen Frosh
Birkbeck College, University of London, UK

© Peter Emerson and Stephen Frosh 2004, 2009

First published 2004
This edition published 2009 by
PALGRAVE MACMILLAN

Palgrave Macmillan in the UK is an imprint of Macmillan Publishers Limited,
registered in England, company number 785998, of Houndmills, Basingstoke,
Hampshire RG21 6XS.

Palgrave Macmillan in the US is a division of St Martin's Press LLC,
175 Fifth Avenue, New York, NY 10010.

Palgrave Macmillan is the global academic imprint of the above companies
and has companies and representatives throughout the world.

Palgrave® and Macmillan® are registered trademarks in the United States,
the United Kingdom, Europe and other countries.

ISBN-13: 978–1–4039–0568–0   hardback
ISBN-13: 978–0–230–59540–8   paperback

This book is printed on paper suitable for recycling and made from fully
managed and sustained forest sources. Logging, pulping and manufacturing
processes are expected to conform to the environmental regulations of the
country of origin.

A catalogue record for this book is available from the British Library.

A catalog record for this book is available from the Library of Congress.

10 9 8 7 6 5 4 3 2 1
18 17 16 15 14 13 12 11 10 09

Printed and bound in Great Britain by
CPI Antony Rowe, Chippenham and Eastbourne

Contents

List of Tables and Figures

Tables

Figures

Acknowledgements

Although this book is primarily methodological in scope, our extensive use of material from one research 'participant' also gives it the feel of a detailed case history. For this reason, we would like especially to acknowledge the contribution to our work of 'Lance', whose willingness to participate in the research interviews reported here provided the necessary conditions under which our narrative analytic procedures could be developed. We would also like to thank the Local Authority who gave permission for the interviews to take place. Parts of Chapter 1 are adapted from S. Frosh (2004), 'Psychosocial Studies and Psychology: Is a Critical Approach Emerging?' *Human Relations*, 56 (1547–67).

1

Introduction – Psychosocial Studies and Critical Narrative Analysis

The developing and so inevitably contested field of psychosocial studies has been characterised as 'a chain of speech acts; that is, something communicative; a name for a currently enlivened phrase invoked by people doing interesting work who might want to talk with each other' (Burman, 2008: 6). This discursive view makes room not only for research based on collaborative agreements but also for the tensions of strong disagreements capable of contributing to reflexive questioning and to generating diversities of theory and practice. In the first edition of this book (2004) our positioning of critical narrative analysis in the broad 'communicative' context of psychosocial studies served both to historicise and engage with a range of theoretical and methodological debates affecting narrative research. Our aim was to provide a trail of accountability for choices we made both in relation to theorising our clinical research base and in establishing a fit with some innovative applications of critical narrative analysis, which we then demonstrated. We particularly welcome the reissue of our book in paperback because we hope this will make more easily available for students and other practitioners a contribution to narrative research intended from the start to be practical as well as stimulating to further theorising and application. We welcome it also as an opportunity to re-engage the narrative of our own text with some recent developments in the fields of psychosocial studies and, of course, narrative research. The body of the text itself, offering an incremental and extended demonstration of critical

1

narrative analysis, has not needed reworking, but we believe continues to resonate with a range of current psychosocial and narrative research debates and directions.

The psychosocial subject

There once was little doubt that psychology should be thought of as the 'science of behaviour' and hence that it would aspire to the seeming rigour of the natural sciences and, especially, be able to distance itself from the arts. This lofty ambition has turned to air, despite repeated attempts by psychologists to establish fully fledged scientific credentials – notably, these days, through neuroscience (which might indeed be scientific) and evolutionary psychology (which assuredly is not, if a respect for evidence and scholarly argument is a hallmark of the scientific worldview – Rose and Rose, 2001). What has become increasingly apparent is that psychology is a broad discipline, largely but not solely empirical, very fuzzy at the edges where it merges with sociology, biology, brain science and the humanities, and just as much a discursive construction as any other area of knowledge. Enough Foucauldian-inspired scholarship has now flowed under the bridge of academic and clinical psychology (e.g. Henriques *et al.*, 1998; Rose, 1999) for it to be well established that psychology emerges out of a set of perceptions of individuality and 'selfhood' which in turn are connected with the power of particular constructions of social reality – for example, the belief that there is such a thing as a bounded human subject, the biology and psychology of which (or whom) are closely entwined and which can be studied as a coherent object of knowledge.

The empirical tradition is still dominant within psychology, partly for political reasons (it pays to have a discipline registered as a science) but more because of the continuing influence of the modernist vision of progress through technological advancement. Knowing more, controlling more fully, intervening with more power – these are not only the aspirations of the drugs industry, but also of the broader range of psychologists, who can be thought of as basically on a voyage of discovery and conquest. Yet what is apparent is that while maps of the brain may be becoming more accurate and interesting, and artificial intelligence more intelligent, on the whole psychology does not develop in a linear way, uncovering mysteries once and for all as it proceeds, but cyclically and allusively, sometimes producing insights, not infrequently influencing the ways in which we conceptualise ourselves, and often returning roughly to where it started. In so doing, much psychology acts rather like the humanities in deepening perception rather than in accumulating knowledge; it is also very much like other social sciences, increasing local understanding without making a giant, universal step forward.

There are a variety of issues emerging from this. First, psychology is a branch of activity that has its own ideological and hence political investments – rather a different point of view from the one adopted by those who claim for it some kind of 'scientific neutrality'. Not only has psychology been used actively by governments from time to time, but it is also part of the state apparatus for selection, categorisation and treatment – as witnessed in education and health as well as management, policing and the military (e.g. Burman, 1994). More subtly, the emphasis on the individual as the object of knowledge is an approach making specific ideological claims, which can be seen most clearly in assumptions about the relationship between what is individual (seen as 'personal') and what is social. In particular, the strict division between 'individual' and 'social' risks the Scylla of reducing one to the other (so that, for example, the social is seen as no more than the free interactions of individuals, or the individual is seen as fully constituted by her or his social class, or gender or 'race' position) and the Charybdis of essentialising each element so that the social is 'bracketed off' in discussions of the individual, or vice versa. It is because of our wariness concerning assumptions such as these that we set the context for our work in this book in what has come to be called *psychosocial* studies, reflecting an interest in the psychosocial as a seamless entity, as a space in which notions which are conventionally distinguished – 'individual' and 'society' being the main ones – are instead thought of together, as entwined or possibly even the same thing. This is a difficult procedure, raising numerous problematic issues, most notably that of how to think oneself out of the position in which the psychological and the social are intrinsically separate, without losing the capacity to think at all. In other words, is there something intractable in each of the two parts of this fused-together whole, so that if one dispenses with what is a disciplinary pre-given ('individual' or 'society') one is left clutching thin air?

Because psychosocial research of this kind shares in the (largely poststructuralist) enterprise of examining the conditions for knowledge out of which disciplinary power arises, it offers critical leverage on psychological theories and practices. This is a key strategic point if psychosocial studies are to hold onto an awareness of the socially and historically constructed nature of the discipline of psychology as a whole, and of its 'object of study', the psychological subject, in particular. The expectations of this 'leverage' in relation to the development of psychosocial studies, however, continue to be highly contested and cannot be taken for granted. Debates range from concerns about essentialist 'new threats of social or psychological reductionisms' (Burman, 2008: 3), through questioning how 'crucial' (Hoggett, 2008: 6) or perhaps 'heuristic' (Jefferson, 2008: 4) is the difference between the psycho and the social. Frosh and Baraitser (2008: 4) propose adaptation of the Lacanian metaphor of the 'Moebius strip', a blurring of the 'psychic' and the 'social' as 'inside and outside flow together as one' suggesting that 'the choice of how to see them is purely tactical'. Wetherell (2008: 80) judges that the persistent dualism of 'psychic/social distinctions' continues to 'plague the study of subjectivity and identity'. Nevertheless, from the perspective of a critical approach to psychology, it is apparent that psychological work cannot be construed as merely 'problem solving', the term given by Kuhn (1970) to scientific activity which takes place within accepted boundaries, when the general paradigm for what is valuable in a discipline is uncontroversial. It is well attested in social, historical and discursive explorations (e.g. Henriques *et al.*, 1998), and is lived out in the experience of working in academic psychology departments, that psychology has a specific history relating to particular conditions of emergence which have made it what it is, and that underneath a spurious surface of accepted norms (for instance, the scientific paper model for measuring good work) there is turmoil. The sheer abrasiveness of encounters around genetics and evolutionary psychology, or the legitimacy of psychoanalysis, or the relevance of feminism, or the history of psychology's involvement with racism, suggests that what is going on is a struggle between different ways of conceptualising psychology, rather than simply the best strategies of experiment and investigation.

A *critical* approach means taking this struggle seriously, seeing it as indicative of the actual problem of psychology, rather than a technical nuisance because the best methods have not yet been worked out. For instance, Frosh and Baraitser (2008: 1–2) argue that the emergence of the field of 'psychosocial studies' has 'created an opportunity for the re-insertion of psychoanalysis into the social sciences' – although, as Wetherell (2008: 73) suspects, this could also be seen as a more general movement towards 're-inscription of interiority'. Frosh and Baraitser note that this has 'not been uncontroversial', with long-running debates, as Wetherell notes, 'since the late 1980s' (2005: 170), focused largely around the relative merits of differing understandings of 'subjectivity/identity' and 'agency/intentionality'. In these debates, discursive psychology is positioned from a performative perspective to 'analyse agency as a discursive resource' (ibid.) and is critical of psychoanalytic attempts to go 'beyond language' to 'inner experience' in contrast to psychoanalytic claims that discursive accounts of individuals' identity positions suffer from a social determinism and can better be accounted for in terms of 'psychological processes', notably 'the unconscious', affecting the individual's emotional investment in particular discursive positions. More recently, these debates have led to critical questions about the kind of psychoanalysis that might be appropriate to psychosocial studies, or as Hook (2008: 6) puts it, 'what version [of the unconscious] might best suit both psychoanalysis and psychosocial studies' – debates involving professional tensions at times recommended in terms of 'mutual suspicion that is generative' (Burman, 2008: 5), at others perhaps better described in terms of 'giving and taking offence' (Baraitser, 2008). For example, the discursive critique of psychoanalysis, that it has 'no elaborated theory of language as a practical activity' (Wetherell, 2003: 107), can be seen to be taken up in Parker's (2005) theorising of a 'Lacanian discourse analysis in psychology'. This, in turn, is now being carried forward by Frosh (2007) and Frosh and Baraitser (2008) in narrative analytic work drawing on Lacan, that remains sympathetic to discursive psychology, in part through the re-inscription of a 'social notion of the unconscious' (Hook 2008: 7), thus distancing itself from Kleinian contributions to psychosocial research, in particular, and arguing for more 'tentative' and 'bottom up' rather than 'expert system' and 'top down' interpretive strategies. From a critical psychosocial perspective, that is, all psychological work requires constant examination for what it reveals of relations of power and dominance, assumptions over 'human nature', and the connections between what is taken to be 'psychological' and what (conventionally, the 'social') is not.

This critical stance becomes especially significant because of the contribution psychology itself makes to the construction of its own subject; that is, because psychology deals with human subjects as its topic of study, its claims to knowledge are themselves exertions of power. This manifestation of 'reflexivity' can be seen particularly clearly in the history of psychological theories on 'race'; the use of psychological 'expertise' to generate social policies is also relevant; more generally, the ways in which people construe themselves owes a lot to influential psychological theories, perhaps particularly psychoanalytic and biomedical ones (it is worth considering here, for instance, how the label ADHD now applies, or how people routinely use sexual repression or notions such as 'trauma' or 'acting out' as explanations of their own or others' behaviour). Contemporary subjectivities are to a considerable extent governed by the perceptions of psychology, particularly where claims to scientific status are made and accepted. Conversely, psychological theories draw strength from the 'common sense' (i.e. ideologically inscribed) assumptions and ways of symbolising experience prevalent in the culture. Exploring the manner in which psychology becomes a resource for meaning-making in everyday life, and the significance this has for people's understanding of themselves and the world, is part of the broadly critical agenda of a psychosocial perspective, linked as it is to the general argument that the human subject is made in and of social processes.

Qualitative research methods

Psychosocial studies have ingrained in them an effort to recover or construct meanings; that is, they work in a terrain in which interpretive work is given priority. This involves an assertion of the value of interpretive, qualitative methods (some of which have a long history in other orthodox social sciences such as anthropology), despite difficulties in establishing stability and generalisability of findings. These issues have been discussed very fully by feminist and other qualitative and critical researchers (Henwood and Pidgeon, 1992;

Smith, 2003); the key point here is that qualitative research is part of a major shift affecting the social and psychological sciences which has contributed to the erosion of the hegemony of traditional empirical science in determining what counts as knowledge. This includes advocacy of a constructionist rather than representational paradigm for understanding language; that is, because experience is constantly produced in language, research becomes concerned with gathering and analysing discursive forms, talk and text.

Qualitative research methods have become influential in psychology and other social sciences to a degree which would have greatly surprised researchers 10 or 20 years ago. Taken as more than a methodological convenience, qualitative research methods go to the heart of some of the key issues in establishing a psychosocial approach. McNamee (1993: 4) points to this when she characterises the difference between positivist and poststructuralist approaches to social science as 'a difference between the representational and the constitutive views of language'. In the former, explanations and descriptions '*represent* what is actually there'. Constructionist theory, by contrast, argues that 'reality' is relationally constructed, that 'participants in context create the realities within which we live'. Because 'ways of talking *construct* our worlds, the discursive forms...that emerge and gain viability within particular communities become our primary data' (ibid.: 5). Research in this context becomes centred on narratives of various kinds, embedded in the relatively naturalistic ways in which people express themselves.

Work by qualitative psychologists has shown that some discursive forms sustain more viability in certain socio-historical contexts than others, which suggests that what counts as 'knowledge' is not neutral but is ideologically invested (Gergen, 1994), and that the social construction of meaning is closely allied with power (e.g. Foucault, 1977, 1980). An example here is the way feminists have questioned the social and subjective authority of such power through problematising gender relations and masculinity. For instance, Wetherell (1992: 4–5) pays particular attention to how 'sense-making and the interpretative building blocks from which people construct their accounts are bound up with issues of power and social practices'. Gender identity, she suggests, is 'a version of subjectivity...constructed through discourses and certain social practices' redolent with ideological debates. Therefore, analysis of the primary data of people's text and talk can be expected to demonstrate the discourses they draw upon, how these construct or constitute available identities or subject positions and prevent or marginalise others, and what issues of power and social practice are bound up with them.

The most popular form of qualitative research of this kind to have emerged in social psychology in recent years is discourse analysis, particularly of a kind inspired by Foucauldian theory (Potter and Wetherell, 1987; Willig, 2001). Discourse analysis is concerned with texts, often but not necessarily derived from interviews, placing emphasis on the socially derived axes that underpin the discourses of individual speakers. The assumption of 'discursive psychology' is that language is performative, acting particularly as rhetoric to establish a point of view; that is, language functions to persuade, constructing its positions as it goes along. Part of this persuasive process is to produce accounts establishing the power of one meaning position over another. To do this, interpretive repertoires (a term sometimes used interchangeably with 'discourses') are drawn on, which derive power from the way in which they are culturally embedded, particularly if they are not questioned, as widely accepted assumptions can be used to 'warrant' a particular discursive act. Discourse analysis represents an attempt to provide accounts of the underlying assumptions which act as kernels of everyday rhetorical activity. Gee (1992: 108) thus describes discourses as 'ways of displaying (through words, actions, values and beliefs) *membership* in a particular social group or social network', such that discourses discipline people by apprenticing them, forming associative links and 'folk theories common to the group'.

Some discourse analysts, calling themselves 'discursive psychologists', have been more interested in the ways in which the language used by speakers promotes particular arguments or engenders certain effects. For example, Edwards and Potter (1992: 27) define their work as 'a *functionally oriented approach* to the analysis of talk and text', the aim of which is 'a better understanding' of social activities. They are concerned to answer variations on the core question: What actions are performed or accomplished by this piece of text/talk? Edwards and Potter (1992: 28–9) summarise the key elements of discursive analysis as: (a) attention to discursive content in terms of its social function; (b) concern with 'action', that is with how 'people perform social actions' through spoken and written language; (c) scrutiny of how this action is accomplished by drawing on various resources of language, style, rhetoric; (d) expecting that, since talk/text are understood as functionally oriented, variability of accounts indicates constructed differences serving different contexts; (e) concern both with 'the rhetorical (argumentative) organisation' of talk/text and with how possible alternative version(s) are being countered; (f) special interest in 'how cognitive issues of knowledge and belief, fact and error, truth and explanation, are dealt with'. Following this tradition and drawing on positioning theory (e.g. Harre and Moghaddam, 2003) in the context of discursive psychology, Wetherell (2003) proposes the need 'to develop concepts for understanding and describing those individual repetitions in meaning-making in emotional and relational contexts that become defined as "character" or "personality" or as "symptoms" in conventional psychological terms' (ibid.: 117), that is, concepts she describes (Wetherell, 2008) as 'psycho-discursive practices'.

It has been argued that despite having contributed hugely to the resurrection of psychology as a discipline dealing with personal meanings, discourse analysis has various drawbacks from a critical perspective. One concerns the tendency, especially in Foucauldian-inspired discourse analysis (Willig, 2001), to restrict interpretive work to revealing the discursive elements (usually called something like 'cultural' or 'interpretive repertoires' – Potter and Wetherell, 1987) drawn on by people when warranting their views or actions. This approach has shown itself able to offer documentation of the existence and pervasiveness of such 'underlying' discursive elements, but it is debatable how much has been achieved here in addition to what might already have been derived from sociological analysis. For example, Wetherell and Potter's (1992) exemplary study of racism in New Zealand first offers a historical analysis of how certain discourses concerning Maoris have arisen, and then shows how they operate to govern the accounting practices of white New Zealanders. The analysis here is fascinating and important in demonstrating that powerful social discourses actually construct consciousness, but it also tends to present the individuals concerned as 'judgmental dupes', without offering insight into the personal dynamics which might make these discourses so salient for the individuals concerned. However, more recent discursive work, such as Wetherell's mentioned above (2003, 2008), suggests substantial development in the proposal to 'make sense of both the cultural resources for identity work and in vivo identity performances' by making 'psycho-discursive practices the unit of analysis' and employing a range of forms of investigation, including narrative analysis (2008: 80). The inclusion of narrative analysis here may help to address what has been a second concern, that 'discourse discourse' is potentially conservative, performing no movement from analysis to social action (Burman, 1992; Parker, 1992); that is, it shows the functioning of social discourses without providing leverage to consider how people might assert agency in their lives. In particular, as we will argue, narrative analysis offers theoretical positioning and methodological resources capable of contributing precisely in Wetherell's words (a) to researching 'the person as ... a site where meaning gets organised' (2003: 114), and (b) both to 'an understanding of the patterned discursive practices of social interaction' as well as warranting a 'sense of how narrative and meaning-making work as social action' (2008: 79), (c) thus serving to 'analyse agency as a discursive resource' (2005: 170) and able to privilege individuals' voices, choices, contradictions and irresolutions as well as the relational constitution of identities through personal narratives.

Our own interest in the *psychosocial* subject has led us to attempt to hold onto the critical gains of discourse analysis, with its roots in social understanding, but combine it with a focus on the active constructing processes through which individual subjects attempt to account for their lives. This has led us to look to *narrative analysis* as a qualitative approach in which the political/value dimension is very significant. Our suggestion here is that its capacity for close attention to the social construction of subjectivities in relation to dominant discourses, and its potential for reflexive openness, make narrative analysis a specific discourse methodology capable of critically contributing to the interplay between personal and social change (Riessman, 1993, 1994). Manning and Cullum-Swan (1990: 465) give a useful definition here, linking the idea that narrative is central to personal sense-making with an appreciation of how the construction of individual narratives – the process of 'storying' – is linked to social discourses and takes place in a firmly interactional or intersubjective context.

The emphasis in contemporary anthropology and feminism is upon the study of lives from the narrator's experience, as a shared production with social scientists. These stories are seen as real, yet with a tenuous grip on a consensually defined social reality that can be validly and reliably reproduced by social scientists. Emphasising the role of these narratives in empowering persons through more subtle understandings of their life situations stands the structuralist concern with the power of codes, rules and social formations of texts on its head. To a striking extent, narrative analysis is rather loosely formulated, almost intuitive, using terms defined by the analyst. Narrative analysis typically takes the perspective of the teller, rather than that of society...If one defines narrative as a story with a beginning, middle and end that reveals someone's experiences, narratives take many forms, are told in many settings, before many audiences, and with various degrees of connection to actual events or persons. Thus themes, principal metaphors, definitions of narrative, defining structures of stories (beginning, middle and end) and conclusions are often defined poetically and artistically and are quite context bound.

There are many issues here that need to be addressed when considering the 'critical' utility of narrative analysis, and which will be returned to at various points in this book. For example, defining a narrative as something with a 'beginning, middle and end' raises the question of whether what is being focused on is a kind of 'defensive' structure in which the actual disorganisation of everyday life (its 'beginning, *muddle* and end') is being denied. Narrative as 'fiction' serving defensive or functional ends is rather different from narrative as representation of 'reality'. Riessman (2008: 188–9), however, rethinking the balance of her earlier attention to 'text-based coherence' in the process of 'demonstrating trustworthiness' or validity of interpretation focuses on 'disrupted narratives', personal narratives particularly related to trauma, characterised by 'incoherence in the testimonies, reflecting fragmented lives'. She argues that 'simplified closure' or in effect a foreclosure or appropriation of 'coherence', may be the result of 'listeners' (and investigators') need for continuity and meaning' (ibid.: 190), suggesting instead another kind of interpretive listening that is not (quoting from Schiff and Cohler, 2001) 'to a single coherent voice of purpose but to the existence of meaning and non-meaning together' (Riessman, 2008: 190). This challenge to how both 'coherence' and 'defensive' assumptions may affect the utility of narrative analysis appears to support our critical attention below to the interpretive importance of recognising and not appropriating contradiction, irresolution and absences/struggles around, for instance, possible emergent social and/or personal alternative narratives/discourses. Drawing on Ricoeur, Mishler (2006) is critical of how 'narrative analysts with clock-time perspective tend to favor a master narrative that gives unitary, coherent meaning to our lives'; in contrast, he proposes the need for 'a relational theory of identity, one that locates the recurrent restorying of our lives within the flux of contradictions and tensions of the several social worlds in which we are simultaneously actors and respondents to others' actions' (ibid.: 42), a perspective that may help to resist the culturally normative 'preference of tellers' and 'interviewers ... and narrative analysts' for 'well-formed stories' (ibid.: 46) and instead engage with 'fractured accounts, which do not have the shape of our culturally expected and preferred stories' (ibid.: 45). Burck (2007), from a clinical perspective, specifically links critical narrative research efforts 'not to strive for coherence' with possibilities to 'avoid appropriating an individual's meaning-making and agency', which in turn she suggests could help to 'form the basis of a different definition of evidence-based practice'. Frosh (2007), also in connection with trauma (p. 640), critiques assumptions of 'narrative coherence' and 'the tendency to produce integrated "narratives" of experience' (ibid.: 637, 639). Frosh and Baraitser aim to resist the risk of reducing psychoanalytic interpretation of text to a formulaic identification or the coherence of a 'pre-existing grid' (2008: 13), in part by utilising critical narrative analysis in the context of Lacanian attention to the idea that 'language often references its own "aporias", its own gaps into which aspects of experience fall' (Frosh, 2007: 640). This, in turn, raises a continuing broader thematic question central to this book and concisely put by Phoenix (Andrews *et al.*, 2008: 65): 'how to analyse narrative contexts and whether or not it is warranted for analysts to orient to the wider context if narrators do not'. Nevertheless, when narrative analysis goes further than simply identifying what stories are being told, it gives a prominence to human agency and imagination that suits studies of subjectivity and identity. In particular, it is argued that personal narratives often emerge around people's experiences in their lives of breaches between ideal and real, self and society (Bruner, 1990). These claims, because they suggest possible locations or sites for meaning-making work, may have special importance to the narrator and special interest for critical research. The narrative processes constructing coherence in the face of such breaches and/or constructing ways for keeping the coherence of the narrated event open to question, have implications for personal meaning-making through the ways people talk that have material effects in terms of subject positions and 'membership', of fitting or not fitting in with dominant forms of social life. Narrative analysis thus offers a methodology particularly sensitive to subjective meaning-making, social processes and the interpenetration of these in the construction of personal narratives around 'breaches' between individuals and their social contexts.

Exemplifying critical narrative analysis

Not a survey or a manual, but a stimulus and an invitation

It will be evident to readers of this book that we do not survey the whole field of narrative analysis, but rather offer a version of it that differs from, say, that of other researchers who have chosen a more thematic approach to uncovering stories in texts (e.g. Murray, 2003). However, two recent overviews of developments in narrative research (Riessman, 2008; Andrews *et al.*, 2008) help to briefly underscore a number of key themes structuring this book. We are sympathetic to the idea of 'good enough narrative research' criteria (Riessman and Quinney, 2005: 391). This on the one hand helps to resist the temptation of one best version by making room for complexity that can be described as 'narrative research's incoherence' (Andrews *et al.*, 2008: 3), for 'diverse forms' of practice reflecting 'diverse theories and epistemologies' (Riessman, 2008: 1) including realist, postmodern and constructionist strands (Riessman and Quinney, 2005: 393). On the other hand, it encourages reflexive engagement in definitions, in determining a relatively coherent narrative of its own professional boundaries. As we have seen above, even the effort to define 'narrative' is fraught with implications. Nevertheless, in view of the 'tyranny of narrative' under which 'the term has come to mean anything and everything' (ibid.), we broadly agree with the view that 'what distinguishes narrative from other forms of discourse' can be focused in terms of 'sequence and consequence: events are selected, organized, connected, and evaluated as meaningful for a particular audience', and hence the focus of analytic attention on 'how and why events are storied, not just simply the content to which language refers' (ibid.: 394). A related development, evident from the diversity of narrative research projects across Andrews *et al.* (2008) and, building on Mishler (1990), strongly supported by Riessman (2008), concerns the theme of 'validity' or 'trustworthiness'. Arguing that in contrast to quantitative research, qualitative research 'has evolved different standards' of 'reliability and validity' (Riessman and Quinney, 2005: 407), and pointing out that 'validity and ethics are products of the paradigms that spawn them', Riessman (2008: 185) suggests: 'The validity of a project should be assessed from within the situated perspective and traditions that frame it (which, ideally, an investigator makes clear up front).' On this basis, she proposes that 'trustworthiness' in narrative research is best served by 'the work of building a corpus of diverse exemplars' (ibid.: 200), 'candidate exemplars of various analytic approaches' (ibid.: 18). Whatever the 'paradigms', however, a methodological refrain is that the analytic work 'is grounded in a close study of the particular', a process that is typically 'slow and painstaking, requiring attention to subtlety' in language use (ibid.), and is characteristically in support of a theoretical/ethical commitment to 'search for ways to return authority to narrators' (Andrews *et al.*, 2008: 154). While this encourages an expectation and respect for 'many versions', we agree with Riessman (2008: 48, quoting Temple) that each interpretation must be anchored in 'something within the text'.

Our suggestion is that the fine-grained method of analysis we promote offers a way of counteracting the tendency to impose upon, or 'ascribe' to, texts pre-given meanings arising out of professional or expert discourses, thus contributing to a range of efforts to recognise and account for a reflexive interpretation of the research relationship itself that also includes the reminder 'to accept the inescapable limitations of our research findings and theories' (Mishler, 2006: 47). Keeping close to the detail of the material makes for more careful grounding of claims in the context of what is actually said. However, we share Gee's (1999: 5) view that 'whatever approach we take, it holds out the hope that various micro-communities of researchers working in diverse fields can begin to come together...contributing to a "bigger picture"'. Mishler (1995: 117) cautiously offers a typology of models of narrative analysis under the broad headings of: reference and temporal order; textual coherence and structure; and narrative functions. His argument is that there is no 'one best' approach, but rather a need for more 'inclusive strategies that would provide a more comprehensive and deeper understanding both of how narratives work and the work they do'. Staging a debate relating to the 'limitations of interpretation', Frosh and Emerson (2005) argue for the importance of 'reflexive engagement around professional assumptions and positionings' (ibid.: 321), which becomes all the more important in a climate of 'inclusive' or 'collaboratively binocular accounts' (Frosh and Young, 2008: 2), if only because inevitably 'all interpretive research ... involves the application of some pre-set theoretical concepts' (Frosh and Emerson, 2005: 309). This kind of syncretism may involve, for example as with Hiles and Čermák (2008), co-ordinating of a range of methodological activities into a narrative research 'orientation', including in this case an interpretive level drawing specifically on the kind of critical narrative analysis presented in this book. It may involve the kind of broader co-ordinations of disputed theories and methodologies, as for example we have referred to above (Frosh, 2007; Frosh and Young, 2008; Frosh and Baraitser, 2008); as well as include (some version(s) of) narrative analysis amongst a range of other qualitative research approaches, for instance as in Wetherell (2008: 80). It may also draw on co-ordinations of 'narrative therapy principles' (Riessman, 2005: 396; Hiles and Čermák, 2008) with narrative methods of research, making potential contributions, as Burck (2007) suggests, to 'a different definition of evidence-based practice', 'systemic research', and to therapeutic conversations. Riessman (2008) and Andrews *et al.* (2008) provide many further diverse examples, any or all of which may offer 'possibilities of collaboration (if not corroboration)' (Frosh and Emerson, 2005: 323). In terms of Mishler's typology, our book may be broadly situated as paying attention to both textual coherence and structure, and to narrative functions. Our aim is to introduce and demonstrate an approach to critical narrative analysis emphasising reflexive attention to 'fit', in the sense of constraints and opportunities, between theory, method and application or utility, with a view to promoting contextualised, close textual analysis over extended stretches of textual material. Our illustrative choice of 'clinical' focus (sexually abusing boys) for textual analysis, as described below, is purposefully situated with this 'fit' in mind.

Part and parcel of this kind of 'fit' includes theoretical and methodological reasons for choices of sources and kinds of possible narrative texts. We discuss this in more detail below in relation to our use of the narrative research interview. In broader terms, we note that Potter and Hepburn (2005) have argued 'for moving away from the use of interviews' in favour of more use of 'naturalistic materials' (ibid.: 281) in qualitative research. They suggest a range of 'contingent problems' and 'necessary problems' associated with qualitative research interviews. While it is beyond our scope here to review these, we suggest that rather than constituting reasons for avoiding research interviews, these may better serve as a helpful aide memoir, in effect, for promoting the importance of 'skilled interviewing' (Andrews *et al.*, 2008: 152) and greater alertness to reflexive interpretation of the research relationship. Riessman (2008: 23–4) observes that '(m)ost narrative projects in the human sciences today are based on interviews of some kind', and reviews attitudes and skills helpful to achieve 'detailed accounts' that include '(e)ncouraging participants to speak in their own ways'. Hiles and Čermák (2008: 151) argue that a narrative orientation is 'a methodological approach in its own right', and recommend, as do we here, drawing on Mishler's (1986; 1991) 'narrative interview' conceptualised precisely not as an 'interrogation' but 'a mutual exchange ..., a site for the co-production of narratives' (ibid.: 151). While we agree with Potter and Hepburn (2005: 290) that appropriate transcription of such interviews should show 'interviews as interaction', we agree with Mishler's (2005) criticism of their tendency to assert one best form of transcription. This appears to ignore the relatively widespread agreement amongst researchers that 'there is no universal form of transcription suitable for all research' (Riessman, 2008: 218), but rather 'there are many different notation systems', each involving its own 'theoretical assumptions about language', and that transcriptions themselves are inevitably 'forms of representation that serve rhetorical functions' (Mishler, 2005: 317) and thus 'deeply interpretive' (Riessman, 2008: 29).

Thus, this book is not a manual for narrative analysis, but we hope it will stimulate ways of thinking, and further 'inclusive strategies', engaged with critical perspectives and practices. We invite the reader into an analytic process of generating a situated, partial and warrantable *psychosocial* 'knowledge', the increasing importance of which is clearly suggested by the observation that, '"The story" turns out to be an especially vital point of intersection among work in many different fields' (Brody, 1998: xiv). Our textual analysis is presented as illustrative of our approach and not comprehensive of what might be construed even from the given texts we subject to analysis, let alone from sexually abusing boys as 'a population'. Nevertheless, we argue that attention to the narrative/discursive construction and positioning of and by the psychosocial subject serves to link accountability and 'moral identity'. The capacity of critical narrative analysis to explore the generation of this kind of accountability recommends it as an approach respectful of the agency of persons negotiating 'possible lives', particularly in the context of breaches of dominant discourses or canonical narratives where possibilities for alternative or replacement personal narratives may serve to warrant new meaning-making and different social practices.

Individual lives and social concerns

Our argument for the utility of narrative analysis for a critical qualitative psychology rooted in psychosocial studies includes a claim that the intense scrutiny of individual accounts is an activity worthy of research attention. Whereas many discourse analytic studies have been concerned with tracing the impact of cultural discourses on talk as revealed in texts derived from numerous research participants, critical narrative analysis of the kind described in this book is founded on the detailed investigation of very small numbers of research 'subjects', whose processes of accounting and making sense of their experience is seen as being of intrinsic interest, rather than as a source for generalisations. That is, narrative analysis does not use a 'sampling' procedure (Mishler, 1996), but asks specific questions about particular lives: how does this person, in this context, get to give the account she or he does, how is it constituted, what does it do, what psychological processes can be seen at work in it? It may be that the narrative processes at work can also be observed in others, but that will be an empirical question. One thing linking critical narrative analysis with some other disciplines, such as psychoanalysis, is thus the assumption that the important issues in people's lives are highly specific, however strongly they might also relate to their status as social beings. The 'psychosocial' approach here means attending to the very specific location of any particular subject at the junction of social and personal investments and concerns.

For this reason, we have chosen to introduce our methods in this book through an extended example of one young man, known as 'Lance', who was interviewed as part of a project on sexually abusive young men. This choice of subject is not a complete accident, but reflects the use of qualitative research methodologies to enable attention to be paid to how participants drawn from clinically or socially 'difficult' populations construct or make sense of their own development, behaviours and experiences, especially where, for example, patterns of abuse of social norms are both subtle and highly intransigent. In our example, how does a sexually abusive boy make sense of his sexually abusive behaviours? How does he see his sense of self, of masculinity, of others and of relationships? On what bases and through what processes does he make choices leading to and maintaining the sexual abuse of other children? How can the interpenetration of this boy's personal narratives and canonical (i.e. widely shared) cultural discourses be read so that agency and accountability neither dissolve into radical relativism nor remain merely individualistic and pathologised, uncritically examined in the legal, treatment and media frameworks of dominant narratives? Research insight into such areas of meaning-making may have important clinical implications for engaging collaboratively in treatment or therapeutic work with this boy and others sharing the characteristics of marginalisation or opprobrium.

Underlining again the critical importance we attach to theoretical positioning and methodological choices in relation to field of research, and to the constitutive power of dominant discourses to privilege some but restrain other approaches, it is worth recognising that, for example, a feminist understanding of the 'contested nature of masculinity' (Edley and Wetherell, 1997: 204) may itself be thought of as a discourse still resisted and marginalised by the dominant trends of professional understanding, practice and priorities in the field of sexually abusing boys. We have suggested elsewhere (Emerson and Frosh, 2001) that practitioners in this field who argue that even a preliminary interrogation of 'how is it that normality permits sexual abuse to be so prevalent?' has yet to start (Postlethwaite, 1998: 34), are up against a powerful consensus of influential assumptions supporting the institutionalisation of responses to sexually abusing boys from the perspective of a professional optimism that sees the field 'on the brink of formalising and clarifying the work of the past few years' (Ryan and Lane, 1997: 198–9). From a feminist perspective, consolidation of the field without re-theorisation around gender fails to address the central problem of sexual abuse: the social construction of masculinity, and the many 'ideological debates' surrounding it (e.g. MacLeod and Saraga, 1988). Furthermore, from a social constructionist perspective (e.g. Gergen, 1994), re-theorisation includes challenges to the dominant theoretical assumptions and (principally quantitative) research methodologies of traditional empirical science considered foundational to the 'formalising and clarifying' of the field of sexually abusing children and adolescents. Thus, our theoretical perspectives are used in effect to problematise prevailing professional views. In essence, we suggest that the individualising and pathologising accomplished by the formulation of sexual abuse in terms of 'dysfunction' mask the ways in which canonical narratives by which boys are 'apprenticed' to become men, and dominant subject positions of masculine identity, contribute to the involvement of men in violent and, in particular, sexually abusive activities.

Thus, theoretical reframing of our particular field of research makes room for different questions and the possible generation of different 'knowledges'. Our argument in this very specific context is that discourse and particularly narrative analysis can supply theoretical and methodological tools helpful in researching abusing boys whose accounts may be viewed *both* as triggered by breaches with, *and* as instances of, dominant social discourses. These tools provide ways of focusing attention on narrative forms of male marginalisation, specifically the accounts of boys who sexually abuse other children, in order to explore discursive means by which this behaviour makes sense. The argument then becomes that such abusiveness constitutes one of the 'possible lives' sustained by our gendered array of cultural meanings and particularly available in the situating of masculine identities. If the male majority in sexual abusing is framed as an exaggeration of prevailing norms of male dominance, then critically regarding both those norms and how they interpenetrate and structure personal narratives of boys who sexually abuse other children, must include a simultaneous awareness of social context and of subjective identities, and of how contextually available discourses or narratives enable some accounts but constrain others.

Our overall ethical and methodological aim was to pay research attention to subjectivity and meaning-making, to how these boys make sense of their sexually abusive behaviours in terms of self, other and relationships. We have argued elsewhere (Emerson and Frosh, 2001: 89) that 'focusing through language on "how their viewpoint is built" or on "the power to name reality", represents a "tectonic" shift in relation to the field of sexually abusing adolescent and younger boys, away from accounts of their behaviour in "historical context" to "transformations of discourse about behaviour".' We discuss below, as central to our approach to narrative analysis, theoretical and methodological implications of recognising the interview as discourse and the act of transcription as inescapably interpretive.

A particular point which the present book does not explore in detail, is that concerning the gendered (un)differentiation of abused 'children'. It may help, therefore, to briefly address the question whether in our choice of, and attention to, the 'male monopoly' in relation to 'boys who sexually abuse other children', we have ignored or elided gender relations and thus made them invisible. In our reframing of the fields of research and treatment of sexual abusers discussed above we have argued that 'the contested nature of masculinity' (Edley and Wetherell, 1997: 204) may itself be thought of as a discourse still resisted and marginalised by dominant trends of professional understanding, practice and policies. Our aim has included both taking into theoretical account and putting into methodological practice the feminist challenge that the first step towards a distinctly feminist theory is 'a recognition of gender as a centrally important feature of child sexual abuse: the gender of the perpetrator rather than the victim' (MacLeod and Saraga, 1988: 23). This centralising of 'the male monopoly' has been both recognised and fudged in the field of sexual abuse. For example, on the one hand it is recognised in descriptions of 'the modal sexually abusing youth' that 'the vast majority of currently identified youth are male (91 to 93 per cent)' (Ryan and Lane, 1997: 6), a finding that continues to hold (e.g. Erooga and Masson, 2006: 4). On the other hand, the literature is littered with a range of typically ungendered descriptors, which include 'sexually abusive youth', 'adolescent sexual abuse' (ibid.), 'sexually aggressive children' (Araji, 1997), and more recently 'children (and young people) with sexual behaviour problems' (Johnson and Doonan, 2005; Erooga and Masson, 2006). In fact, female adolescent sexual offenders are considered to represent only 'between 2–7% of adolescent sexual offenders' (Morrison and Print, 1995: 7), an estimate in line with Robinson (2005: 175) who nevertheless reports an 'increase in girls entering the judicial system for sexual offending'. While figures for sexually abusing children suggest 'that among very young children males and females were about equally represented' (Araji, 1997: 122), Araji also notes that 'preadolescent female sex offenders' appear not to go on to offend in adolescence and as adults (ibid.: 84), although Ford (2006: 164) broadly asserts 'there is no clear answer to the question' whether 'sexual abuse perpetration in childhood predict(s) a life time of sexually aggressive activity'. However, a clear driving force behind the proliferation of treatment programmes is precisely the professional belief that 'the average adolescent (*sic male*) sex offender, who does not receive treatment, will go on to commit...sexual crimes' as an adult (Morrison and Print, 1995: 7), and that unless the 'child perpetrator' (*sic male*) is treated 'the community' and he are at risk of his progressing 'from less serious to more serious sexual offences' in adolescence and adulthood (Johnson, 1988: 227, and Araji, 1997: 87). We labour this point to underscore the challenge that remains (Emerson and Frosh, 2001: 88) to be addressed, in treatment as well as in research contexts, of critically centralising 'the gender of the perpetrator rather than the victim'. To some extent this has begun to be addressed under, for example, the rubric of 'groups within the population – attending to diversity' (Erooga and Masson, 2006: 4–6), which includes gender along with age, ethnicity, learning disability, and is directly linked with 'service provision'. However, while this draws important attention to a range of factors affecting research and treatment, in relation to gender per se it appears to invite the field to embrace a further developmental essentialism rather than grapple with questions around 'the contested nature of masculinity' (Edley and Wetherell, 1997: 204). For example, Robinson (2005) rightly argues that assessment needs to consider 'gender differences ... (b)ecause the development and socialization process of females and males differs' (ibid.: 175). She then cites significant feminist work by Gilligan (e.g. 1982) and others (e.g. Jordon *et al.*, 1991) proposing that 'females derive their identity through their relationships and connections with others' (Robinson, 2005: 176), in contrast to 'research on male development (that) indicates males tend to develop their identities through independence, separation and autonomy'. In support of 'research on male development' Robinson cites Erikson, whose work Gilligan and others strongly challenge not only on grounds of its pejorative and pathologising male-as-norm application to girls and women, but also to problematise its hegemonic construction of boys and men. That is, there is a danger here in the field of sexual abuse of simply offering an essentialed female developmental model (e.g. Scott and Telford, 2006) to sit alongside an essentialist male hegemonic model, rather than using the critical leverage of the former to further historicise/contest 'the nature of masculinity'.

In their discussion of 'victims and abusers', Glaser and Frosh (1993: 13) state that 'surveys have shown a preponderance of girls over boys among victims of sexual abuse', a view supported more recently by Robinson (2005: 180) who states that '(p)erhaps the most consistent and striking finding for sexually abusive female juveniles, is the high rates of victimization they have experienced compared to sexually abusive juvenile males', and which Ford (2006: 164) suggests may help to explain why studies of 'preschool children with sexual behaviour problems ... found a higher proportion of girls (65%) than boys (35%)'. The 'discovery' (Johnson and Doonan, 2005) of preadolescent and even preschool children who sexually victimise other children has not substantially altered this view although, in the wake of feminist challenges, there is greater awareness of the sexual abuse of boys (e.g. Lew, 1988), including the suggestion that 'whilst the majority of victims of juvenile sex offenders are female (69–84 per cent), as the age of the victim decreases, the victim is more likely to be male' (Erooga and Masson, 2006: 8). In relation to abusing adolescents and children, Morrison and Print (1995: 9) suggest an average difference of age between abuser and abused of 'about 6 years with male victims generally younger than female victims'. The politics of this observation, so to speak, in the context of 'the male majority', has fuelled concerns about 'the possibility that sexually abused boys, in the near term, become perpetrators' (Watkins and Bentovim, 1992: 239–40), although, more recently this view has been challenged by research suggesting the importance of other 'risk factors' and that 'sexual victimization per se (is) neither a necessary nor sufficient condition for sexual perpetration' (Williams and New, 1996: 125; Araji, 1997: 44; Skuse *et al.*, 1998; Johnson and Doonan, 2005: 36), indeed, that 'being abused is far from being a predictive factor in becoming abusive' (Erooga and Masson, 2006: 10).

We have argued elsewhere in relation to abusing boys, 'that a feminist perspective informed by a social constructionist stance provides the means for exploring links between the construction of boys' masculine identities and the choices of some boys to implement sexually abusive practices.... Feminist foregrounding of masculinity in relation to sexuality and violence raises questions about the extent to which sexual abuse represents an enforcement of social–sexual norms *constitutive of* masculine identities rather than their "aberration" ' (Emerson and Frosh, 2001: 82). The observation mentioned above of average difference of age between abuser and abused (boys 'generally younger than female victims'), may contribute to the view that power differences, including gendered discourses authorising and sustaining these, for example, by means of '(t)he use of power-based behaviours or thoughts' (Ryan and Lane, 1997: 85), not only contribute to 'the male majority' but also to processes of grooming or selection of 'victim', where gendered choice of the victim is characterised more by hierarchy than sexuality per se. UK research on a non-clinical sample of schoolboys aged between 5 and 11 years summarised findings that describe 'boys in the primary setting as searching for understanding of gender roles, relationship and power dynamics as well as sexuality' (Lenderyou and Ray, 1997: 9), and make the further suggestion that preadolescent and younger adolescent '(b)oys experience a high level of peer pressure to lose their virginity at an early age...as the best way to "become a man". Boys and girls perceive first sex in very different ways, a sense of regret from girls and a sense of achievement from boys' (ibid.: 4). Articulated in the context of child sexual abuse, the gendered differences in these experiences are likely to include different sensemakings and available or proscribed subject positionings, including those of both abuser and abused.

In summary, behind our gendered attention to 'boys who abuse' is a theoretical and methodological range of choices, principally informed by feminist and social constructionist challenges to researching and responding to the field of sexual abuse, which views the gender of the perpetrator as centrally important to accounting for the sexual abuse of children in our society. This is not to say that the gender of the 'victim' is irrelevant, however, even though this has not been our focus in the material presented here. Indeed, research designed to elicit and explore narrative sense-making specifically around gendered 'choosing' of abused children could be both of interest and of practical utility, not in terms of typologising 'victims' or 'risk factors', but of exploring discourses and psychosocial practices constituting such choosing in terms of available and possibly alternative subject positions of gendered 'victim' identities. In our research subject Lance's material, to take just one example, there is evidence of an attempt to articulate the effects of his abusiveness on a specific boy in relation to gendered assumptions about emotional expression, when he comments that this boy seems not to be finding it 'very difficult' but may be 'just bottling it up...and he's hurt more than he shows'. Not only does this reflect certain stereotypic notions about masculinity, but it may also be an exertion of power (Lance has succeeded in *hurting* the other boy) or even an indirect comment on Lance's own state of mind. Exploring the detailed resonance of 'choices' of victim in this way is clearly in line with our encouragement of research taking seriously both the specifics of an individual's sense-making and the social context (with its attendant assumptions) in which this sense-making takes place.

Lance in our research context

Lance was a 16-year-old white British, 'working class' boy, living at home with one older sister, his mother and father. At the time of our interviews, he had just completed his 'GCSE' examinations and was hoping to find a job as well as continue his education at a local college. He was known to, and had been receiving, court-ordered therapeutic services from Social Services because, in his own words,

'I sexually abused...several boys' over the past five or six years. He volunteered as one of a small group of sexually abusing boys willing to participate in a research project (Emerson, 2000) involving two audiotaped one-hour semistructured interviews with each boy. The first interview was 'Offence-specific', the second organised around the themes of 'Self, Relationships, Gender' with a view to hearing about 'other parts' of the boy's life in order to get a bigger picture; each was thematically organised around a series of core questions designed in the hope that they would elicit personal narrative material. Our textual material used in this book to exemplify critical narrative analysis is drawn from these two interviews. Our analysis of this material contributed to the principle claim of the overall research project, which may be summarised by the conclusion that approaching these boys in ways that give priority to, and thus make more room for, personal narrative accounts, (a) makes more available the kinds of textual material that can contribute to understanding in their own words and from their own points of view how they make sense of themselves and their behaviour, and (b) illustrates the social discourses, beliefs and assumptions that may be organising and sustaining these accounts. Thus, it is argued, personal narrative can offer a critical window on processes of social construction of gendered identity that, in relation to sexual abuse, have two apparently contradictory functions. On the one hand, they sustain the 'male monopoly' of abusiveness; but on the other hand, they may also show signs of, or resources for, resistance or alternatives to a boy's apprenticeship to discourses of abusive masculinity.

Awareness of researcher reflexivity strongly suggests the importance of engaging research participants not only in interviews intended for primary analysis, but also in follow-up conversations reflecting on these interviews and on interpretive feedback from the researcher(s). From a feminist point of view, for instance, Reinharz (1992: 19) argues that '(r)eceiving feedback from interviewees... enables the self-disclosing researcher to continuously correct the interview procedure'. In our research, at the point of preliminary contact and discussion with each boy around informed consent, a third, reflective follow-up interview was proposed to be arranged some weeks after the second meeting to offer feedback to the boy on our own sense-making and to 'hear whether this makes sense to him', as well as to invite any further comments, corrections or observations. Locating participants at this remove in fact proved difficult; however, we were able to recontact Lance. A detailed discussion of his third interview is beyond our purposes here; nevertheless, we can offer an impression of some of his ongoing preoccupations and concerns with a view to contextualising the first and second interview texts drawn on in our exemplifying analysis below, and to providing some narrative and ethical 'closure' on our relationship with Lance. In particular, it gave us some indications of how he retrospectively experienced the first and second interviews, and also how he carried forward a number of key themes and difficulties marking his present experience and inflecting his future intentions and expectations.

For example, towards the end of the third interview, PE (the interviewer) asked Lance about 'any spin-offs at all from the other interviews, either negative or positive'. Lance explained that he found the interviews thought-provoking: 'when I've gone home after the interviews, I've, you know, I have actually sat down and thought about the questions'. Although a veteran of many kinds and contexts of interviewing (e.g. police, social workers, therapists, courts), Lance also stated that 'you've asked questions which I didn't ask...myself, so it's, I don't know, you know, a challenge to think of the answers' – a challenge which, we suggest, his narrative engagement and agility richly demonstrate in the texts discussed below. In response to ethical concerns clearly identified and prepared for at the initial stages of each boy's invitation to participate in the research project, namely how to respond and what to do if the interviewee found the discussions disturbing during or after an interview, PE wondered if Lance's thinking about the interviews caused him any 'trouble or distress', to which he replied, 'I didn't notice any, um, negative parts of the interviews'. While the face value of this comment is significant, it also, we suggest, reflects Lance's skills and ability to make discursive choices affecting his own positioning and use of the interviews; that is, he felt 'in control' for most of the time, but he also was claiming that nothing particularly 'negative' (perhaps meaning difficult or disturbing) was discussed. A further point of importance to Lance, knowing from the start that the interviews were part of a research project, was seeking reassurance that 'when you do this paper' he would remain anonymous in the context of our co-constructed confidentiality. In particular, he reminded PE that 'you said you were going to give different names' and wanted his own trust to be affirmed by a clear 'No' to the question: 'if, you know, if somebody who knew the offences and knew me or...was working with me...saw the paper...would you tell them, if they asked...would you tell them what parts...?'

In terms of discursive themes reflected on in the third interview, in effect carrying forward and inflecting Lance's preoccupation with 'where I am going to go from here', these may be summarised as: (a) some effects of his sexual abusing on and hopes for his mother, himself and at least one boy (a neighbour) he abused; (b) trust; (c) past and further therapy and (d) gender identity issues and choices. At the point of our interviews, Lance had had an enforced 'break' from his therapeutic work with Social Services 'because they, in fact they felt that they couldn't get any further'. He found this 'an opportunity' for thinking 'more than I was when I was there' because, he explained, 'it's a case of while I was going there, that, when I weren't there at home, it's a case of "Well, I'm going there, you know. I don't need to think about it right now, that's all right" '. The substance of this thinking, carrying some implications for his future, may be suggested in that Lance had 'told them I wanted to carry on' and 'they were then willing to carry on with the therapy lessons'. He became aware of the effects of his abusing on his mother, how 'by the offending... I trapped her...Where she, she daren't go outside in case anybody knows'. He experienced similar constraints on his life, limiting things he could do, recreational and educational, because of 'the people I offended with living around...and their parents', and organising his movements so that at 'a certain time I won't go out of the house' in order not to meet a neighbourhood boy he abused. Thinking about this boy, Lance reflected that though 'looking from what he do...he don't seem like he finds it very difficult', he wonders 'whether he's bottling it up...and he's hurt more than he shows...which is more than likely'. Overall, 'looking back' raises for Lance a critical theme of trust, both related, for instance, to how his abuse has affected the boy's parents who 'aren't going to trust anyone...putting them in doubt of what they are', but centrally raising a dominant question for himself, 'how can anyone trust me again?' He illustrates this theme with narratives expressing fear of being 'accused', suspected of being 'up to anything', having made it impossible for his mother to 'start building' trust 'because she lost trust in me because of the offences', of Social Workers and others 'not believing the answer I give' and not knowing 'what I could do to prove to them...that I do want to stop', and feeling stuck because 'they see someone for what they were, not for what they want to become'.

These, and other 'trust' narratives, at the point where our contact with Lance is ending after the third interview, may suggest a positioning of himself in terms of a psychosocial future experienced as uncertain at best and an impasse at worst, expressed in terms of an unresolved dilemma around available relationships and possible identities: 'if other people can't trust me...why should I really trust myself...?' This question seems to place the hope 'to be like everybody else' beyond reach because, at this point at least, he remains unclear about what signs others need to see to trust not only that he knows 'I have two paths...not abusing and abusing' but also that he has 'moved a bit down one path...not abusing'. Lance's subject positioning around available and alternative masculine identities is intimately bound up with these dilemmas and reflections. In particular he expresses a distancing from forms of hegemonic discourses of masculinity identified, for instance, with 'football...or the latest car', as well as practices, illustrated by (albeit with loyalty to) his father who 'likes to prey on other people's fears' and who 'acts the hard type'. In stating rather categorically that 'I'm bound to be different from my dad when I grow up', Lance identifies what he prefers instead in relational terms associated with his mother. He 'would like to be able to get involved more with other people's discussions' and, a theme strongly emerging through our textual analysis below, rather than 'march ahead' or 'barge ahead' like his father, he 'would like to sit down and plan things first'. His own local and culturally mediated awareness that 'society's changing all the time...men are starting to stay in the kitchen and a small amount of wives...go out to work', clearly inflects his sense-making with possibilities of alternative masculine identities which, in terms of moving 'down one path (of) not abusing', preoccupy both how he is 'looking back' and his uncertainties about 'where I am going to go from here', which includes his moving beyond participation in our research project.

Structure of the book

The following chapters each introduce certain theoretical and methodological aspects of critical narrative analysis that are then employed in approaching increasingly extended stretches of text. Chapter 2 is organised around the question of whether the interview questions are bringing forth the kind of material the participant wants the researcher to hear and the researcher wants to analyse. To examine this in principle, we consider the issue of 'the unit of analysis', focusing as an example on a short piece of text from Lance's 'Offence-specific' interview. It is shown that methodological choices have a significant impact on the ways in which the sense-making activities of the narrative material are interpreted and that this in turn affects how or indeed whether the ways 'the culture "speaks itself" through the individual's story' (Riessman, 1993: 5) may be heard. In this instance, the researcher's analytical efforts to privilege and not appropriate the boy's offence related meaning-making include a critical determination to interrogate and prevent premature closure around organising assumptions of gender and power. In Chapters 3, 4 and 5 our analysis is extended to a longer stretch of text transcribed to reflect the interview as discourse. After introducing particular aims and issues, each chapter demonstrates the potential of extended, coherent and critical narrative analysis, developed illustratively across three consecutive parts of Lance's overall response to one question in the second research interview. Broadly, we grapple with the important methodological commitment that, in order to give weight to the participant's meaning-making, the presence of ideological or canonical narrative material in an interview must be interpreted in light of linguistic cues as to how the text was *said* in the context of the interview as a 'co-construction'. With both theory and utility in mind, we argue that attending to the ways in which the boy articulates his perceptions and experience, *increases* critical interpretive access to links between how he actively situates himself through personal narrative, for instance in relation to accountability, and what canonical narratives may be employed in this. This also enables consideration of the extent to which the 'dominant' discourses may warrant his account or be resisted by it, possibly in favour of contesting, potentially 'alternative, "replacement discourses", that fuel positive social constructions' (Henry and Milovanovic, 1996: x).

In Chapter 3, in the context of the research interview as discourse, we demonstrate how the ways a text is said can provide 'micro-' and 'macro-' cues raising interpretive questions that help to privilege speakers' sense-making and to resist 'ascriptivism' (i.e. the tendency of researchers to impose specific interpretations upon, or ascribe meaning to, texts), and that can begin to generate closely warranted thematic interpretation across extended units of analysis. In Chapter 4, we pursue the theme of 'bottom up' interpretation with particular attention to discursive constructions of gendered identities. We demonstrate how persistently fine-grained narrative analytical work can respectfully negotiate the discursive 'messiness' of narrative co-construction, resisting impositions of 'top down' coherence or order, and instead enable engagement with the complexities of discursive subject positioning, of multiple, mixed and simultaneous intentions, understandings and feelings, in relation to the constraints and possibilities of canonical narratives. In Chapter 5, we explore the way in which narratives can be examined in terms of relationships between more 'molar' parts of the material, with a view particularly to identifying effects of cultural discourses. We argue that the use of macrolinguistic transcription tools can offer a transparent warrant for acceptable interpretations across extended stretches of text precisely because they emerge from engagement with and respect for discursive cues to 'meaning sense' in how the text was *said*. We suggest that narrative analysis of text, building on how it was said, can offer a fine-grained, thickly warranted rendering of sense-making in which the narrator's view is not appropriated and the researcher's critical position is neither compromised nor made dependent on an imported expert interpretive framework for professional sensemaking. Thus, for example, we suggest that narrative analysis enables Lance to be heard as a reliable, vital authority in his accounts of himself and of his sexual 'offending', in part precisely because it helps draw attention to his own reflexive evaluations of 'possible lives' and gendered subject positions in relation to hegemonic and potentially counterhegemonic discourses constitutive of masculine identities.

In Chapter 6, we systematically review and pull together themes and issues raised in the course of the book, outlining a model of narrative work as a critical and co-constructive practice capable of closely warranting interpretive work across extended stretches of narrative material, privileging the 'voice' of the respondent/ participant while attending to the 'trace in the text' of canonical as well as potentially counterhegemonic narratives. Our aim in this is to encourage readers to try for themselves investigations using 'inclusive strategies' of narrative analysis in their own studies of 'how narratives work and the work they do' (Mishler, 1995: 17), making their own contributions to the generation of situated and warrantable *psychosocial* 'knowledge' from a critical perspective. The book concludes addressing a number of broad counterclaims and contestations affecting our positioning and practice of critical narrative analysis.

2
Questioning and Transcribing: How to Gain Access to Personal Narratives

Aims: is the interview question eliciting the kind of material that interests the researcher and in what ways is it available for narrative analysis?

The process of narrative analysis begins with the issue of collecting narratives in ways that allow participants to thoughtfully talk about the issues with which the researchers, and hopefully the participants themselves, are concerned. This is most commonly achieved through a relatively 'open' form of interviewing, which aims to target a set of research questions whilst also allowing for flexible and 'rich' talk. This chapter is organised around the reflexive question of how to establish whether the interview questions are eliciting the kind of material the participant wants the researcher to hear, and the researcher wants to analyse. To examine this, we consider the issue of 'the unit of analysis', focusing as an example on a short stretch of text from an interview with Lance, a 16-year-old boy who has sexually abused a number of children. We show that methodological choices have a significant impact on the ways in which the narrative material is interpreted, and that this in turn affects how or indeed whether the ways 'the culture "speaks itself" through the individual's story' (Riessman, 1993: 5) may be heard. While this assumes the researcher's responsibility to theorise and select areas of interest, it also highlights a key impulse informing the methodological and ethical/political challenge of our critical narrative approach, to resist

'ascriptivism' (Wilkinson and Kitzinger, 1995: 108): 'to find ways of working with texts so the original narrator is not effaced, so she does not lose control over her words' (Riessman, 1993: 34). In this instance, the researcher's analytical efforts to privilege and not appropriate the boy's meaning-making include determination to interrogate and prevent premature closure around organising assumptions of gender and power. Further aims of this initial narrative analysis are: (i) to consider the relation between transcription and interpretation; (ii) to compare two ways of 'reducing' narrative texts for interpretation; (iii) to argue for an interactive understanding of the interview as discourse (Mishler, 1986).

Beginning with beginnings

The interview we are drawing on here to illustrate our argument is conceptualised as a Narrative Interview Guide comprising certain introductory points followed by a series of seven 'open' core questions. Although the purpose over the interview hour was not necessarily to cover all these questions, initial analysis included paying attention to whether, for example, the interview allowed enough time for the boy to comfortably pace his entry into the conversation and for the researcher to be satisfied with the quality and quantity of the resulting text at the levels of content, process and texture. Through an initial analysis of Question 1 (Q1), we demonstrate how we began to substantiate our overall impression that the interview questions elicited personal narrative material of interest to the researchers and clearly available for critical analysis.

Q1 reads: 'Some people are describing you as a boy who sexually abuses other children. In your own words, how would you describe this kind of behaviour?' The aim of this question was from the start to generate conversation with Lance in ways that would privilege his perspectives and processes of sense-making in relation to the researcher's focus on sexually abusing boys. The interview was not geared to invite inventories of specific sexually abusive behaviours, to obtain, for example, the kinds of quantitative and 'objective' accounting suggested by 'scientific research' or expected in assessment or court reports.

In practice, Q1 was not delivered or read, but constructed through conversation. In order to initiate and maintain a focused yet dialogical approach, PE (the research interviewer) drew on a number of conversational practices including checking out his own questions, reflecting back responses, floating possibilities, normalising, tracking, recycling the core question in various ways, refining the core question to pick up on related emerging words and themes and maintaining neutrality in the senses both of not taking 'a certain position' and of curiosity (Cecchin, 1987). Moving on from certain introductory remarks (e.g. underlining issues around informed choice, purpose and focus of the interview and limits of confidentiality), PE situates Lance in relation to the interview and first question: 'I'd like to ask you to begin with to talk as much or as little as you might want to.' The idea here is to invite him not to say more than he wants to so that what he does say is respected as significant and construed as legitimately under his control. While the interview context in practice empowers the interviewer to ask certain questions, it should not *disempower* participants from exercising choice in when, how much and in what ways they 'talk'. Further developing this context, PE introduces assumptions of subjectivity and multiple perspectives: 'You may have a different idea in your understanding about that than other people do.' The aim here is to underline the invitation for this participant to express his own views 'about how you see things, how you say things, how you think about them in your own words', even if, or precisely because, they may differ from others' views. The assumption that participants have their own ways of making sense of things not only intends to respect their views but to support what can be described as a therapeutic approach to 'collaborative conversation' (e.g. Fausel, 1998) that fits with research commitments to resist effacement or appropriation of participants' voices. This is the case even though it is also recognised that in many situations various forms of decision-making (e.g. concerning personal responsibility and social justice issues around abuse) may remain to be made (Byrne and McCarthy, 1995).

Initial reading of the raw text of Q1 suggested that the development of this question across this portion of the interview did elicit content and process issues both of interest to the researcher and available for narrative analysis. That is, Lance stays focused on meaning-making responses to the question and develops these through a series of personal narratives. But this was by no means obvious at first, either during the interview or for some time after. Before presenting our initial analysis of Q1, we will reflect briefly on the researcher's own experience of the interviewing process.

A research 'epiphany' after first interview and during first reading of the raw first transcript

The experience of the first interview with Lance raised a number of points. Some were very practical, like either keeping to the declared hour or negotiating another 15 minutes. Others raised broader, more ominous questions. Throughout the interview, PE noted afterwards in his informal research diary, 'I kept on asking myself, "Where are the personal narratives? How can I get Lance to tell a story?" and doubting whether my questions were doing what I had hoped for, that is, I'd "ask" and he'd "tell". I am left wondering why it doesn't look more like the textbook examples of narrative responses – left wondering "Where is the story?"'

The process of typing the raw transcript from the audiotape did little initially to help answer these questions. It was arduous, time consuming and made PE acutely aware of 'holes' in the text where he could not decipher the spoken words, sometimes even his own. He sensed a paradox in his responses during typing: while accepting that the raw transcription was falling far short compared to the face-to-face experience of the interview itself, yet he listened with a compulsion to somehow produce a word-perfect typescript. It felt like falling between two stools, the transcript neither reflecting the 'real' experience nor constituting a seamless whole of the spoken words. No stories plus a suspect text felt like a bad beginning.

Some way into the transcription, however, a bit of light began to shine around some obvious differences between the language of the Interview Guide governing the interview and that of the interview itself. The Guide was written in 'complete sentences', whereas the interview proceeded with, to be generous, a very flexible kind of grammar and construction. For example, following on from PE's introductory remarks (described above), he initially constructed Q1 (quoted above verbatim from the Guide) as follows across this stretch of raw text (numbers are line numbers from the transcript):

55/PE: OK, so if, if we start, and what I'd like to do is ask you to begin with to talk as much or as little as you might want to, ahh,

about this, it was just that some people are describing you as a boy
who sexually abused other children.

L: Uhhu.

PE: Umm, and, in you own words, what I'd like to know is how do
you describe this kind of behaviour, how, how do, I mean, what is
the, if somebody says 'Lance is a boy who sexually abuses other
children', what does that mean to you? Does that make sense as a
question?

L: Yeah.

PE: Yeah? So you may have a different idea in your understanding
about that, than other people do.

72/L: Well, um, I've, well, sort of like thoughts when I um (?) other
people to commit sexual acts.

PE: Right.

L: Umm, whether it be forcing physically or to um

PE: Uhhu

L: ...um to do sexual acts which I want him to do...

PE: Uhhu.

85/L: ...and they, um, and they did not, or were not old enough
to make the decision themselves.

Despite its 'messiness', this flexibility of conversational language
made mutual sense in the flow of words, thoughts, references and
rapport that composed the interview relationship, as even Lance's
opening responses, with his own grammatical style, show. PE began
to notice, for example, that this language made room both for his
own 'nerves' and for Lance's, and to see how the tentative, flexible,
formulating-and-reformulating conversational style (which included
and evolved with the emotional content of the first meeting and of
the subject matter) facilitated the question in the context of the
interview relationship, knitted it into the to and fro of the conversation, rather than fall short of its written formulation. That is, PE
began to see the conversation as the context for the construction of
meaning, rather than a vehicle for simply carrying or representing,
in effect, prefabricated formulations of meaning, either the
researcher's or participant's.

Still, where were Lance's stories, his 'personal narratives'? PE
approached his first reading of the first raw transcript of this first
interview with Lance seriously wondering what to do if no personal

narratives showed up. He began to feel some relief, however, when at least certain themes seemed to emerge, themes he began to catalogue under terms like Origins, Agency, Force, Trust, 'Wrongness'. Of particular interest was the possible theme of 'Desire', which seemed to link with what Hollway (1989) and others have claimed to be the canonical discourse of the 'male sex drive' as something addictive, verging on the natural and uncontrollable. This was suggested from the text in comments such as:

> once I done it ... it's that I enjoyed it, I want to do it again, and, you know, carry it on. (l. 261)

and:

> ... still going on doing it again ... for pleasure ... reasons. (l. 288)

Whilst material like this is clearly available to alternative interpretations (indeed, the existence of alternative 'readings' of data is a basic assumption of all qualitative research methods), the apparent congruence between these comments and a popular social science 'theory' (that men's sexual behaviour is often warranted by appealing to some apparently 'biological' mechanism) was reassuring for PE, who was otherwise sharing a feeling common to many researchers when faced with a mountain of data – that nothing made sense.

Theoretically aware of Gee's (1991) methodology as used, for example, by Mishler (1994: 9) to trace 'primary themes' across narrative texts and summarise them 'in the form of propositions, that is statements of (the narrator's) aims, actions and evaluations', PE felt some excitement when he began to notice: (a) Lance's thematic material seemed to emerge not, so to speak, paragraph by paragraph, but here and there both within the conversational area around each specific Interview Guide question as well as across the entire interview; and (b) themes connected and developed out of one another, informing and interacting with one another, embedded and embedding, giving coherence and shape to Lance's responses across the interview. Noticing the virtual absence of anything approaching a paragraph-by-paragraph response from Lance made it obvious why the transcript did not have the reassuring textbook appearance he had been looking for. In the context of the interview as a conversation themes emerged interactionally. A small 'epiphany' was that, having begun to notice from Lance's text certain themes and their conversational emergence, PE then began to recognise personal narrative material around and in the development of these themes. That is, personal narrative emerged or came into view not as textbook paragraphs but through the interview understood as a form of discourse (Mishler, 1986a, 1991), as organising constructs or 'situated events' (Riessman, 1993: 17) in a conversation itself punctuated by the researcher's core questions. These general observations will be further developed through accompanying textual analysis as we begin to discuss issues relating to transcription, selection and reduction of personal narrative, and to propose a working definition of personal narrative.

Transcription as interpretation – an act of meaning-making

As argued in Chapter 1, changing social science assumptions about the contextuality of knowledge and the inevitability of interpretation underwrite increased attention to subjectivity and the validity of subjective knowledge (e.g. Gergen, 1994). An interest in personal narrative and the co-construction of subject-to-subject meaning-making is anchored in such assumptions (Stivers, 1993). Mishler (1991) argues that the transcription of discourse, including personal narrative, is theory driven, a methodological example of ways in which 'facts emerge as the result of a theoretical perspective' (Gergen, 1994: 201). Gee (1999: 88) argues that 'a transcription is a theoretical entity. It does not stand outside an analysis, but, rather, is part of it'. The act of transcription is not a matter of striving for a text 'more accurate or objective than the other' (Mishler, 1991: 264), but an activity driven by and reflecting the assumptions of the researcher, that is, it is 'an interpretive practice' (p. 255) carrying 'evaluative connotations' (Gergen, 1994: xiv). For example, Mishler (1995) points out that feminist interest in personal narrative is driven by a political determination to privilege the experience and views of women, typically marginalised by cultural 'master narratives' whose 'unexamined and taken-for-granted assumptions about how the world is and ought to be conceal patterns of domination and submission'. He cites personal narrative as an exemplar of Haraway's (1988) feminist proposal of 'situated knowledges' in which all knowledge claims are relativised and the 'privilege of partial perspective' becomes the basis of accountability for subject positioning (Mishler, 1995: 114–17).

This line of argument draws attention to accountability and to the more or less overt roles and purposes of the researcher in the production of knowledge. It is in the context of such ideas that Riessman (1993: 60) asserts: 'Analysis cannot be easily distinguished from transcription.' There is an inevitable movement back and forth between the activities of transcribing tape to text, and developing understandings which are driven by (implicitly and/or explicitly) preferred theories, interests and values. For example, Riessman points out that 'narrative theorists disagree on the importance of the interview context in the analysis of narrative' (ibid.: 20). Mishler's (1995) typology indicates a diversity of approaches and purposes informing the field of narrative analysis. Arguing that there is no one best way to study or define narrative, he recommends developing 'more inclusive strategies that would provide a more comprehensive and deeper understanding both of how narratives work and of the work they do' (p. 117). This understanding that amongst a diversity of discourse approaches 'none of them (is) uniquely "right"', foregrounds researchers' accountability for choices around which 'fit different issues and questions better or worse than others' (Gee, 1999: 5). Our own interest in developing a critical narrative analytic approach to research, and our intention to situate this research in the context of feminist and social constructionist perspectives, clearly informs our approach to transcription. In particular, we share the strong preference for transcription that reflects the joint discursive work or co-construction involved in the emergence of personal narratives during the interview, thus allowing those interactions to be an integral part of the narrative analysis. Even, as below, when making choices to reduce raw interview text to discrete sections for particular detailed analyses, our aim is to focus, for instance, on possible structures of a participant's 'core narrative' without losing either a sense of the rhetorical dimensions of its interpersonal development and interactional work through the interview or an awareness of wider social discourses that may be informing it.

The theoretical complexity and methodological sophistication of narrative analysis suggest a special significance for research with 'clinical', often highly stigmatised, populations amongst whom treatment and therapeutic approaches are largely dependent on the interaction of speakers. Furthermore, as Brody (1998) suggests, because ' "the story" turns out to be an especially vital point of inter-section among work in many different fields', narrative study invites 'interdisciplinary dialogue' (p. xiv). The research 'fit', for example, between a social constructionist stance and narrative theory (Gergen, 1994: xix) also extends to implications and adaptations of these ideas to narrative therapy (e.g. White and Epston, 1990; Parton and O'Byrne, 2000).

Riessman (1993: 2–4) points out that the precise definition of personal narrative is a subject of debate. Her preliminary definition suggests that personal narrative 'refers to talk organised around con-sequential events. The teller in a conversation takes a listener into a past time or "world" and recapitulates what happened then to make a point, often a moral one'. Riessman draws on Bruner's (1990) view that personal narratives are triggered at points of difficulty or trauma in persons' lives and provide a primary way of making sense of expe-rience. In particular, Bruner (1990: 49–50) suggests that narrative involves an effort to 'find an intentional state that mitigates or at least makes comprehensible a deviation from the canonical cultural pattern'; it is, he argues, 'the power of noncanonical events to trigger narrativising' (ibid.: 81). Hyden (1997) further elaborates this view, but specifically in relation to the organisational/legal triggering of professional and at times mandated 'institutional narrative' texts such as Assessment and Court Reports which are typically dependent upon and highly appropriative of personal narrative material inform-ing them. It can be argued that without the wider context or inter-penetration of canonical discourses, without a recognition of what Mishler calls 'master narratives' (1995: 114), personal narrative in the textually reduced context of the discursively isolated individual has diminished meaning.

At many levels a sense of radical 'deviation', covert and overt, psychological and social, self-evident and self-contradictory, sur-rounds the behaviour and experience of sexually abusing boys: the 'triggers' to narrativising (professional and personal) are many. In our research, personal narrative offers a significant focus for an analysis of how these boys try 'to make a point' and to be 'comprehensible' about their dangerous and highly stigmatised abusing behaviour. This approach need not represent a slide into 'moral or political fence-sitting' (Byrne and McCarthy, 1995), but, by beginning with an assumption that narrative is a 'situated event' (Riessman, 1993: 17), it may instead, as Bruner (1990: 25–30) argues, offer a way of unpacking presuppositions or deconstructing commitments that constitute these boys' gendered investments in and accountability for 'how and what (they) know' and do.

An entry into analysis: selecting and reducing personal narrative from raw transcript text – a story of how it is right to keep wrong secret

Riessman (1993: 58) states: 'Determining where a narrative begins and ends and the listener/questioner's place in producing it are textual as well as analytical issues.' Using the text below we illustrate a process of determining where this personal narrative begins and ends. At the same time we demonstrate two different approaches to reducing the narrative text, and then suggest how approaching the emergence of personal narrative as a joint construction, viewing the interview as discourse, is particularly useful for our purposes. The section of raw text reproduced immediately below in Figure 2.1 is typical of Lance's delivery across his two interviews, and comes early on in his response to Q1. As the listener/questioner, PE is actively engaged in maintaining the conversation with Lance, this 16-year-old boy who has, in his own words, sexually abused 'several boys' (l. 102). In stark contrast, for instance, to Mishler's (1994: 7) interview experience of uninterrupted '12–13 minute' narrator responses, at no point during the roughly two hours of Lance's two interviews did he narrate in 'chunks' of more than four or five lines of raw text. Our own personal and clinical and research experience of talking with adolescent boys suggests that an absence of extended monologue is not uncharacteristic – in fact, perhaps the persistence of Lance's actual responsiveness could be seen as more uncharacteristic. But, how can personal narrative be identified in this kind of conversational context?

Figure 2.1 Raw text L1/Q1: ll. 164–225

164/L: Yeah. It's like, um, after every time
PE: Um
168/L: it's a case of Ah, I don't want to do that again, yeah, it's sick, it's wrong,
PE: Yeah
L: you know, you know, again, and then always the next time.

Figure 2.1   Continued

174/PE: Yeah. (2 secs) Where, where do you for yourself get the idea that it's wrong?
L: Um What, where do I get the idea?
PE: Yeah, for yourself. I mean, probably people have told you that it's wrong. For your own self, where do you think the ideas come from that help you decide whether something's right or wrong, whether this particular thing is right or wrong?
184/L: Uh, I just, it's just knowing that I shouldn't be doing that, um, ... with any-one, (2 sec) umm (14 sec). Um, it's a case, you know, I always knew, you know, it was wrong
PE: Uhhu
190/L: I can't remember where I ac where I first got the idea from, you know
PE: Yeah
L: Um, it's one of the things you grow up knowing, I guess.
PE: So where, where the idea came from that it was wrong feels like a long time ago. You don't know where it, where it came from initially?
L: Yeah.
PE: Yeah
203/L: ???So if I knew that early that it seems I knew it was wrong, that's the case why I keep saying I don't tell anybody
PE: Yeah
L: Uh. (3 secs)
PE: So there's a sense of the wrongness makes you want to make it into a secret, is that what you're saying?
213/L: Umm. You know, when most people do something wrong it's kept secret.
PE: Um. Yeah. So it's like a lot of other things that one might do wrong
L: Umm
219/PE: and you don't want other people to know so you make it a secret?
L: Umm
PE: Is that, is that right?
225/L: Yeah.

Note: Inaudibles are marked by ????, pauses by (number of seconds).

An important context of this interview is the researcher's stated interest in 'how you see things, how you say things, how you think about them in your own words' (ll. 42–3). In his response to PE's interest in what it means to him to be described as 'a boy who has sexually abused other children' (ll. 57–8), Lance has already described his behaviour as 'wrong' (ll. 106, 141), as well as being repeated (l. 136, 'after each time'; l. 149, 'when it comes to the next time'; l. 164, 'after every time') and something he desired (l. 154, 'it's some-thing I had wanted'). In relation to the lines in Figure 2.1, PE has become interested in how Lance's view of 'wrong' relates to his repe-tition of abuse (ll. 164–73), and he asks 'where do you for yourself get the idea that it's wrong?' (ll. 174–5). Lance's response loops back to the theme of 'wrongness', which, we demonstrate below, he develops through an identifiable personal narrative providing a canonical motive for secrecy. This narrative can be seen as triggered by PE's question about the origins of Lance's view (l. 174) and finishing as PE checks out his understanding with him, 'Is that, is that right?' eliciting Lance's summary, 'Yeah' (ll. 223–5). So, a story unfolds which is identifiable and to that extent discrete – it has a 'beginning and an end' and can be 'pulled out' of the surrounding text. But, it also links back to preceding themes and will be further elaborated along with others.

Riessman (1993: 17) suggests that '(m)ost scholars treat narratives as discrete units, with clear beginnings and endings, as detachable from the surrounding discourse, rather than as situated events'. We suggest that, while a relatively discrete narrative unit can be constructed from the above brief stretch of text, much of its meaning depends on where it is situated in the conversation, that is, its relation to contributory themes of 'wrongness', desire and repetition. Our preference, therefore, is to see it as a situated event and as one amongst other 'embedded narrative segments within an overarching narrative that includes non-narrative parts' (ibid.: 51).

Labov's framework – the functions of clauses

Following Riessman (1993), having identified a personal narrative section, we draw on Labov's (Labov and Fanshell, 1977) framework for an initial understanding of how the 'story' may be organised. Labov suggested that well-formed stories share basic invariant ingredients and that clauses function in a variety of specific ways: 'to provide an abstract for what follows (A), orient the listener (O), carry the complicating action (CA), evaluate its meaning (E), and resolve the action (R)' (Riessman, 1993: 59). This suggestion involves a retranscription of the raw text organised in terms of how clauses function in the identified personal narrative. In Figure 2.2, we retranscribe the raw text from Figure 2.1: (a) trying to employ Labov's framework – parsing Lance's speech into clauses and identifying the parts of his narrative in terms of their functions; (b) and at the same time reducing the text to a 'core narrative', that is, 'a radical reduction of response to a skeleton plot' (ibid.: 35), keeping the focus on Lance's narrative by deleting all but one of the researcher's responses (which functions in this case as the Abstract for what follows).

Figure 2.2   Core narrative retranscription of raw text L1/Q1: ll. 164–225 from Figure 2.1 using Labov's framework

Orientation
L: Yeah. It's like, um,
after every time

Complicating action/Evaluation
it's a case of Ah, I don't want to do that again,
yeah, it's sick, it's wrong,
you know, you know, again,

Resolution
and then, always the next time.

Abstract
PE: Yeah. (2 secs) Where, where do you
for yourself
get the idea that it's wrong?

Orientation
L: Um … What, where do I get the idea?

Complicating action
L: Uh, I just, it's just knowing
that I shouldn't be doing that,
um, with anyone, (2 sec)
umm (14 sec).
Um, it's a case,
you know, I always knew,
you know, it was wrong
I can't remember where I ac
where I first got the idea from, you know
Um, it's one of the things you grow up knowing,
I guess.
Yeah

Evaluation
So if I knew that early
that it seems I knew it was wrong,
that's the case why I keep saying
I don't tell anybody
Uh. (3 secs)

Resolution
L: Umm. You know,
when most people do something wrong
it's … kept secret.
Umm
Yeah.

Drawing on Labov's framework, a relatively discrete personal narrative can be identified. The researcher's question serves as the Abstract for what follows – that is, by the end of the narrative PE will have an expanded view of the content of his question. At the same time, it is clear that what follows is thematically linked to what precedes this question. Lance's own question – 'What, where do I get the idea?' – Orients PE, as the listener, in at least two ways. First, Lance may be trying out the fit between his understanding of what PE has asked and PE's understanding of what he has asked. Second, he may be questioning the research question to prepare PE for his air of uncertainty. Partly he seems to want to answer PE's question, but also he seems somewhat unsure at this point what he himself wants to say. As Lance develops the Complicating Action (which in this case is not behavioural action but an act of remembered knowing), he does not identify a time before which he did not know 'it was wrong', but rather 'I always knew'. He 'can't remember … where I first got the idea from' because, in effect he suggests, it never wasn't there – 'It's one of the things you grow up knowing'. But there is an implicit complication in this response. His general appeal to a normative 'you' leaves open the question, why, if he 'always knew', did he begin, and why continue? His own discomfort with this complication may be suggested as he concludes this section of his narrative with 'I guess. Yeah'.

The Evaluation clauses are clearly introduced by a summative and consequential 'So' and organised around a logical argument of 'if…' that turns on the implied 'then' 'that's the case why'. What is the argument? Lance is making a case for 'why I keep saying I don't tell anybody', making a case for 'saying' and not saying. On the one hand this case allows Lance to see himself as normal in his knowledge of what is wrong. On the other hand, because there is 'always the next time', the theme of secrecy seems to emerge as a way of not betraying to 'anybody' that what he desires and what he does are, as he 'always knew', both 'sick' and 'wrong'. The argument here seems to link Lance's normative moral knowledge of what he 'shouldn't be doing' to a declaration ('I keep saying') that secrecy ('I don't tell anybody') is understandable and significant. As Lance has identified his moral development as normal, so he brings this narrative response to PE's question (about 'where do you … get the idea that it's wrong') to a Resolution, by moving through his argument beyond the question of origins to a justification for secrecy in terms of what 'most people do'. He resolves the complication of knowing but repeating what is wrong by appealing to a canonical narrative or maxim: 'when most people do something wrong it's kept secret.' Through this narrative, Lance identifies or positions himself as both always like what 'you grow up knowing' and responding to breaches of shared moral knowledge just like 'most people do'.

From the point of view of Labov's framework, Lance's personal narrative makes functional and logical sense. It seems to clearly illustrate what Bruner (1990: 50) suggests narratives do, 'mitigates or at least makes comprehensible a deviation from the canonical cultural pattern'. It enables Lance to openly acknowledge his behaviour as 'sick' and 'wrong' and to openly identify himself with 'most people'. On the face of it, this construction of Lance's raw text almost suggests the logical development of a position statement. This kind of reading, as Riessman (1993: 20) points out, is largely governed by the 'assumption that narrative is the relation among clauses rather than an interaction among participants'. It not only tends to leave out the conversational context of the narrative, but also has largely ignored transcribable linguistic and affective cues such as pacing and emphasis in Lance's response.

Gee's poetic line breaks

Below we examine another way of approaching the retranscription of the same stretch of Lance's raw text drawing on Gee's (1991) use of 'poetic' line breaks based on changes of pitch and 'cues' internal to the text. Riessman (1993: 61) describes her preference for using this approach: 'I start from the inside, from the meanings encoded in the form of the talk, and expand outward.' We suggest this is compatible with Edley and Wetherell's (1997: 205) reflexive characterisation of 'bottom up' approaches to discursive research as geared 'to demonstrate that an analyst's concern … is also a participant's concern within the interaction and present as a trace in the talk before it can be imported into the analysis'. Riessman (1993) argues that whereas Labov's structuralist framework imposes 'external' assumptions (e.g. of invariant 'transhistorical' narrative structures) on the organisation and interpretation of the text, Gee's discursive approach helps to privilege the teller's experience and assumptions 'from the inside' of their own language-use. What differences might be produced by this approach?

Gee (1991: 16) argues that the internal discourse structure of a text, including narrative text, 'functions to set up a series of cues or, better put, interpretive questions'. While answers may be multiple, they are nevertheless constrained in that these questions 'must be answered by any acceptable interpretation'. Thus, 'many answers are ruled out by the structure of the text' (ibid.). The existence of multiple possible interpretations does not constitute *carte blanche* for rampant interpreter 'ascriptivism' or interpretive relativism. The means for recognising such cues and questions is in 'how the text is actually said'. Gee maps the discourse structure of a text in terms of line breaks – paying attention to 'idea units, focuses, and lines' – and in terms of larger narrative units – stanzas, strophes and parts, 'the basic building blocks of extended pieces of discursive language' (p. 23). Importantly for our purposes, this conceptualisation of micro and macro discourse structures, functioning as interpretive 'cues' that privilege the teller's meaning-making, offers a basis for fine-grained 'bottom-up' narrative analysis across very extended stretches of spoken text. Analysing spoken English, Gee argues that 'pitch glide [loosely, spoken emphasis] signals the focus of the sentence', that is, 'the information that the speaker wants the hearer to take as new or asserted information'. Furthermore, any sentence, or portion of a sentence, with one pitch glide is called an 'idea unit'. Thus, '(i)dea units, focuses, and lines are part of the structure of a text which cues interpretation (meaning sense)' (ibid.).

While in the retranscription of our text below (Figure 2.3), we have introduced stanzas, strophes and 'parts' for organising even this brief personal narrative section, we delay discussion of these larger linguistic 'building blocks' for our analysis of an extended stretch of Lance's narrative text in the following chapters. Here, based on multiple listening to the audiotaped interview, slashes separate idea units if more than one per line, capitals represent focuses, and main line parts of the plot are underlined; pauses are identified by, for example (2 secs) and line breaks indicate Lance's pacing of his phrases around pauses or slight hesitations.

Figure 2.3   Core narrative retranscription of raw text L1/Q1: ll. 164–225 from Figure 2.1 using Gee's (1991) 'poetic' line breaks

Strophe 1 (experienced cycle of abuse)
Stanza 1 (don't want what's wrong)

Figure 2.3   Continued

L: Yeah.
It's like (2 secs),
um, <u>after every TIME</u>
it's a case of
AH, <u>I DON'T WANT TO DO /THAT AGAIN</u>, yeah, it's
SICK, <u>it's WRONG</u>,
you know, you know,/

Stanza 2 (repetition of what's wrong)
AGAIN, and <u>THEN</u>
<u>ALWAYS the NEXT TIME</u>

Strophe 2 (origin of moral knowledge)
Stanza 1 (researcher's focus)
PE: Yeah. (2 secs)
Where, where do you for yourself /get <u>the IDEA that it's WRONG</u>?/

Stanza 2 (Lance's focus: always knew)
L: Um (2 secs)
What, <u>WHERE do I get the IDEA?</u>
Uh, I just, it's <u>just KNOWING</u> THAT
um <u>I shouldn't be DOING that</u>,
um, with ANYONE, (2 sec)
umm (14 sec)
Um, it's a case, you know, <u>I ALWAYS KNEW</u>, you know,
it was WRONG/
I can't remember WHERE (2 secs)
I first got the IDEA FROM, you know
Um, <u>it's one of the THINGS you GROW UP KNOWING</u>, I guess.
Yeah.

Stanza 3 (why I keep saying I don't tell)
So <u>if /I knew that EARLY</u> (2 secs)
that it SEEMS /I KNEW <u>IT WAS WRONG</u>,/
<u>that's the CASE WHY I keep SAYING /I don't tell anybody</u>
Uh. (3 secs)

Stanza 4 (normality of wrong kept secret)
Umm. /You know,
<u>WHEN MOST people do something WRONG it's</u>
<u>KEPT SE</u>
<u>CRET.</u>/
Umm
Yeah.

Except for the question that initiates Strophe 2, this core narrative text (like Figure 2.2) omits the researcher from the transcription. It does not read as a joint construction. Nevertheless, within this transcription as influenced by Gee's (1991) framework, the emphasis on how Lance's narrative is said helps to draw attention to affective nuances in the text. There are some obvious parallels between the parcelling up of the text using Labov's framework and Gee's stanzas; and in this case the underlined 'main line' parts of the plot (Gee, 1991: 17) broadly parallel Labov's clausal functions from Abstract to Resolution. However, the attention to internal 'cues' that Gee's framework allows (through pitch glide, focuses and idea units, in particular) helps to amplify a complex mixture of tentativeness and impulsiveness in Lance's speaking which gets lost during the interpretation of the text dependent upon Labov's external categories. While the overall logic of the narrative can still clearly be seen to address itself, in Bruner's words, to finding 'an intentional state that mitigates or at least makes comprehensible a deviation from the canonical pattern' (1990: 50), Lance does this not simply with the logic of a developing position statement, but through a modulation of emotions or emotional investments linked to an appeal 'to underlying propositions that make the talk sensible' (Riessman, 1993: 61).

For example, Strophe 1 can be heard to set the affective tone for the personal narrative of Strophe 2: the foci during Lance's narration of his cycle of abusive relating – time/don't want/wrong/then/always the next time – draw attention not just to a pattern of behaviour he calls 'SICK ... WRONG' (anchored in the tacit, shared assumption that the interview focus is his sexual abusing), but to an emotional meaning for him, the inevitability of 'the NEXT TIME' that 'I DON'T WANT TO DO'. This affective sense of inevitability, of doom, is amplified through Strophe 2. Lance's story of the origins of his moral knowledge as something 'I ALWAYS KNEW' and as developmental ('one of the THINGS you GROW UP KNOWING') is emotionally a story of powerlessness. In the narration of his experience, not only does 'KNOWING' it is wrong fail to prevent what 'I DON'T WANT TO DO', but also there appears to be no outside, no other source of strength to interrupt or resist 'the NEXT TIME'. Is the 'NEXT TIME' inevitable because the inadequacy of Lance's moral knowledge to prevent what is 'WRONG' is central to his sense of himself, thus constraining alternative possibilities for personal agency?

In light of this kind of reading, Stanzas 3 and 4 of Strophe 2 cease to support Evaluation and Resolution phases of the narrative in terms of a secure and defensive appeal to the maxim of a learned, shared and normative use of secrecy. While this appeal is certainly present in the literal meaning of the sentences, the foci of these sentences, we suggest, alert us to a possibly fuller and wider sense of futility in this personal narrative. If Lance's 'if' and 'it seems' represent speculative efforts to make sense of what he suggests he is powerless to control, then his determination to 'keep SAYING/ I don't tell anybody' can be understood as an effort to foreground his telling the truth about something he does which is part of what is 'WRONG', that is, 'I don't tell anybody'. His conclusion in Stanza 4 with the canonical truism from experience, that 'WHEN MOST people do something WRONG it's KEPT SECRET', is not necessarily an appeal to the security of a maxim. The fluency of his opening delivery, 'WHEN MOST people do something WRONG it's', contrasts with the hesitancy of 'KEPT SE/CRET', and the focus words provide a sub-text – 'WHEN MOST … WRONG … KEPT SE/CRET' – which suggests that the normality of wrong kept secret is itself wrong. That is, if this is a solution that 'MOST people' use, including himself, it is nonetheless known and used by Lance to be an intimate part of the inevitable 'NEXT TIME'; if it is a problem, and 'that's the CASE WHY I keep SAYING' it, then what else is there to appeal to in the wider world of social relationships than wrong 'KEPT SECRET'? What other alternative subject positions and practices are available under the dominance of this canonical narrative?

This interpretive reading of the text above suggests an emotionally bleak rather than logically confident personal narrative that, to a large extent, follows from two different approaches to transcription. To the extent that the narrative functions to mitigate his own deviation by trying to make it comprehensible, Lance's narrative does so by implicating what 'most people' do in a cycle of inevitable 'wrong' which the pattern of his own sexual offending adheres to rather than deviates from. The canon of cultural propositions that Lance draws on and that make sensible the statements that his offending is 'SICK' and 'WRONG', also includes the cultural pattern that 'WHEN MOST people do something WRONG it's KEPT SECRET'. In the context of this story, 'ALWAYS' remains a word so extensive that 'ALWAYS the NEXT TIME' and 'ALWAYS KNEW' offer no hope and what 'MOST people' do is already deeply integrated into or constitutive of Lance's cyclical understanding of his pattern of sexual abuse. In this account of his experienced cycle of abuse, Lance situates himself in relation to, rather than in deviation from, a canonical narrative of 'MOST people'.

Riessman (1993) points out that Gee's (1991) framework has the danger of stripping the narrative from its interview context; her own interest in Mishler's (1986a, 1994) view of interviews as a form of discourse, suggests the importance of developing the analysis of personal narrative in this wider context. It is obvious, even in the short transcription we have used for illustration above, that we have not treated this narrative as a literally discrete unit. Thus, in preparation for turning in the following chapter to detailed narrative analysis of an extended stretch of Lance's interview text drawing more fully on Gee's linguistic 'building blocks' but also including the interviewer in the transcription, we will conclude this chapter with some general reflection on a reintroduction from our Figure 2.1 text of two voices (the research interviewer's as well as Lance's) into its analysis.

Jointly constructing personal narrative in the context of the research interview

Following Mishler (1986a), Riessman (1993: 20) recommends that detailed transcription should be expanded to bring the interviewer into the analysis of personal narrative. This, she argues, allows for the examination of 'power relations in the production of personal narratives' and helps to show 'how meaning is interactionally accomplished'. This expansion of transcription and analysis raises new questions, such as, Who asks the questions and with what purposes? and, in this context, What is the teller hoping to accomplish with and through her (his) narrative? The two ways explored above (see Figures 2.2 and 2.3) of reducing and transcribing our raw text, suggest overlapping but also quite different kinds of analysis. Different sense-making is privileged by different transcriptions. The following reflections on our Figure 2.1 raw text, do not offer a detailed linguistic transcription of both voices, but simply aim to illustrate that theorising and viewing the text as a joint construction does add significantly to the possible levels of analysis and interpretation.

We have discussed above efforts we made to develop an Interview Guide and style of conversational interviewing responsive to the challenge not to efface the participant (Opie, 1992). This challenge clearly becomes even more serious in the virtual absence of the person of the participant when all that remains of the interview is an audiotape and the researcher's transcription. Gee's (1991) attention to how a text was said privileges its internal linguistic cues and to that extent serves to help absent narrators retain control over their own words, in part by restraining researcher 'ascriptivism'. In the process of the interview participants maintain more or less control of their own words and meaning-making through their moment-by-moment choices both of how to respond to and situate themselves relationally in the context represented by the interviewer, and of how to respond to create a context for the interviewer's responses. The recognition of this feedback process through an inclusion of the interviewer in the transcription and analysis of personal narratives, requires the interviewer to become more accountable and transparent in terms of their contribution to the conversation, which, in turn, can further support the participant's control over the meaning-making jointly documented in the interview text.

For example, Lance introduces the word 'wrong' earlier in the raw text of the interview as he begins responding to Q1, which PE has just rephrased as, 'if somebody described you to yourself as a sexual abuser, what would that mean to you?' (ll. 99–100). Soon after this he picks PE up on his use of 'circular questioning' (Cecchin, 1987) – 'people always ask those sort of questions ... What do you think other people think ... and I just don't know' (ll. 114–19) – which suggests both that he is an experienced and sophisticated interviewee in his own right (e.g. in police, social work, treatment/therapy settings), and, perhaps, that he wants the research questioning to be addressed more directly. As PE pursues what seems to him an emerging and important theme of 'wrongness', Lance describes a circular pattern of 'the whole abuse' (l. 136) which includes 'abusing', deciding 'that was wrong' and he 'shouldn't have done it', 'but then, straight away, when it comes to the next time, it starts off 'cause it's, well, it's something that I had wanted' (ll. 136–54).

Although, in retrospect, Lance seems to present desire as there throughout, at this point in the real time of the interview PE framed what he heard by a question using the metaphor of Lance being 'somehow pulled back and forth inside of yourself between those things' (ll. 161–2). It is this question that triggers the first line of raw text in our Figure 2.1 above, and Lance reiterates the story of 'always the next time' (l. 172). Holding on to his interest in the theme of 'wrongness', and how Lance may account for this, PE asks about the origins of 'the idea that it's wrong' (l. 174). Lance's response, 'Um, What, where do I get the idea?' may read differently in this interactional context than in either of the analyses of Figures 2.2 or 2.3. In the context of the interview as discourse, the double interrogative (both a 'what' and a 'where') of Lance's question in response to PE's question may suggest some surprise at the tack PE is taking. While PE picks up on 'wrong', has Lance moved beyond or aside from this, offering a cue to his own 'meaning sense' through his new information that 'it's something that I had wanted'? In response to Lance's brief question PE makes an elaborate three-line reply holding to his own agenda which Lance then somewhat haltingly responds to, including an exceptionally long (14 seconds) silence before concluding 'Um, it's a case, you know, I always knew, you know, it was wrong' (ll. 184–6).

Is the question of moral origins the researcher's diversion from a theme of more importance to Lance, that is, desire? In the context of the interviewer's questioning, Lance initially locates the origins of his moral knowledge as always there – 'it's one of the things you grow up knowing' (l. 194) – to some extent thus normalising his own development in terms of 'always' knowing 'it was wrong' to 'be doing that'. But, as PE pursues this issue, asking again about where the idea 'that it was wrong … came from initially' (ll. 196–7), Lance creates a new context for the question. Building on PE's reflective interpretation that it 'feels like a long time ago', Lance constructs a case for 'why I keep saying I don't tell anybody' (ll. 203–4). PE's response of 'Yeah' only leads to Lance's 'Uh' followed by a 3-second silence that, in the context of the dialectic, can be read as an invitation for the interviewer to respond to this new information. In checking out that he understands what Lance has said, PE 'floats' the word 'secret' (l. 211) as a possible synonym for 'I don't tell anybody'. Lance then incorporates PE's word into his own generalisation that 'when most people do something wrong it's kept secret' (l. 213). The function of this comment is, in effect, to close the narrative that for the sake of analysis we have pulled out of its surrounding text.

However, this conversational sequence can clearly be seen as part of a series of 'embedded narrative segments' (Riessman, 1993: 51), as a jointly constructed 'story' nesting in the narrative development of broader discursive themes, including, for instance, that of 'desire'.

We have noted above how our Figure 2.1 text opens in effect with Lance's précis (ll. 164–72) of a preceding cycle of abuse narrative (ll. 136–54) thus serving to introduce and contextualise the relatively discrete personal narrative section we have discussed under Figures 2.2 and 2.3. At the end of this narrative, the theme of 'wrongness' has been developed by its connection to the theme of secrecy; but this theme itself is not developed or further defined at this point. This is partly because the interviewer returns his attention to the other aspect of the dilemma suggested by Lance's cycle of abuse narrative, that is, the theme of desire, by asking 'how is it that they find you doing that even when you're saying that it's wrong' (ll. 254–5) – in effect, how does he account for why he does what is wrong when he 'always knew' it is wrong?

Signs of continuing co-construction and narrative thematic development are evident from two further embedded core narrative sections, Figures 2.4 and 2.5, triggered by PE's questioning following the Figure 2.1 text. It takes PE two or three reformulations of his question to arrive at a version Lance then responds to as in Figure 2.4.

Figure 2.4   Core narrative ll. 257–88

L: Um. I don't know, it's just like, you, you know, once you done it
once I done it,(???)
it's that I enjoyed it,
I want to do it again, and, you know, carry it on.
Umm, so even though every time
I found myself saying it's wrong, you know, not again,
I start to desire it or feelings to do it again
kept overcoming it, um, and it carried on
Um, I don't know, I've kept, I keep remembering, you know,
going, saying, 'You know it was wrong',
then doing it again. You know, it's like every time,
instead of saying, like this, this, it's like every time afterwards
it's a case of saying,
'All right, this is definitely the last time',
but still going on doing it again
for pleasure (???) reasons.

Here, the theme of desire, voiced for the first time in l. 154 (immediately preceding our Figure 2.1 text) strongly re-emerges, reflecting a constitutive sophisticated organisation and interpretation of his experience through the 'male sex drive' (Hollway, 1989: 54) 'master narrative' in which personal agency is dissolved. This social construction of masculine desire as irresistible ('desire ... kept overcoming it') is very familiar to feminists and others interrogating discourses and social practices of abusive masculinity. Wanting to resist closure on this gendered articulation of Lance's experience, and instead responding to it as constituting a dilemma in Lance's life which his interview narrative material itself is an effort to reflect on, PE asks Lance how he makes sense of 'the pleasure reason on the one hand and the sense of its wrongness on the other?' (ll. 290–9). Close attention to how it was said, suggests that Lance's response, in the form of another normative maxim (ll. 302–3), expresses significant ambivalence about this 'master narrative'. However, the broader thematic contrast between 'wrongness' across the Figure 2.1 narrative and desire in the Figure 2.4 narrative raises a further theme of choice. It raises, for example, interpretive questions about cultural discourses of pleasure or desire which, while on the one hand presented as the rationale for the moral paradox of Lance's saying one thing and doing another, as, in effect, the trigger 'to do it again', are also presented as simultaneously constituting available and proscribed subject positions of abusive masculinity.

PE constructs his question, triggering Lance's Figure 2.5 core narrative response, in terms of 'choice' – 'how do you make a choice to go with your sense of what's wrong, or to go with your sense of what you desire?' (ll. 313–16).

Figure 2.5   Core narrative ll. 318–68

L: I think it's a case of picking, you know,
so you in a way make it right to do it
and coming up with reasons
um, ??? I don't know, just going out
and not really forcing them to do it, you know
Yeah, the last ones,
um, they're the ones I'm mainly going on
because they're the ones I can remember ???,
um, it's a case of like every time I start thinking
'Oh, you're going to do it again', you know,
and thinking of reasons why I still could, you know,
it's a case of always thinking about when it first started off
It just started off by the two boys doing it together,
and then asking me to join in.

The 'choice' Lance chooses to narrate is a remarkable feat of reasoning that integrates earlier primary themes in the text. His account
can broadly be summarised as 'coming up with reasons' that 'make
it right to do it' which introduces a new theme: reasoning or rhetoric.
The tentative links Lance has made between 'pleasure reasons' and
'wrong' explain the moral dilemma of his experienced cycle of abuse
in terms of a culturally gendered irresistible desire, in terms of a why,
but they do not explain how. *How* in this Figure 2.5 core narrative is
a rhetorical activity of 'coming up with reasons' that transforms what
Lance earlier called 'forcing physically' (l. 77) into 'not really forcing
them to do it' (l. 327). When PE checks this out with Lance in a question excised from the core narrative – 'So that the situation would
come that you would be creating reasons in your own thinking that
would make you feel that it wasn't forcing?' (ll. 334–5) – Lance twice
confirms his understanding. In effect, these 'reasons' represent a
connection, not a choice between, as PE reflects it, Lance's 'sense of
what's wrong' and his 'sense of what you desire' (l. 315). If the origins of moral knowledge were never not there, the origins of sexual
abuse are to some extent locatable because they are at least discursively connected both with the 'pleasure reasons' and with the
'reasons' that 'make it right to do it': that is, these origins are semi-
nal for learning how to get what he wants, how 'to do it again'
(l. 271). At the level of primary themes developed across this stretch
of text, it can be argued that the moral uncertainty of desire, which
is not resolved simply by the power of desire to overwhelm Lance's
sense of wrong, is being rectified by reasoning or rhetoric. This is not
a reasoning of an abstract kind, but an interpersonal 'reasoning'
capable of handling power in ways, for example, that can skilfully
make force seem 'not really forcing', that is, 'reasoning' that is itself
a form of sexual social practice.

In this section we have suggested, through foregrounding narrative
context and the joint construction of our interview text, how complex processes of sense-making are developed across themes which
emerge and mutually inform one another, serving at times in effect
as 'propositions' that organise and support Lance's 'aims, actions
and evaluations' (Mishler, 1994: 9). To the extent that the personal
narratives embedded in our interview text can appropriately be
described as 'situated events' (Riessman, 1993: 17), we suggest they
are also available for further critical, sociolinguistic analysis

anchored in 'situated knowledges' (Mishler, 1995: 114), those 'partial knowledges' of subject positions both constituted by but also chosen in response to dominant and/or marginalised discourses and discourse practices.

Some conclusions

Using Q1 as a critical example, we have organised this chapter around the preliminary reflexive question, whether our interview questions were eliciting what Lance wanted the interviewer PE to hear, and whether this was what the researchers wanted to analyse. On the basis of our analyses, we suggest this question can be answered affirmatively on both scores. The kind of information we are 'hearing' does interest us and is available for narrative analysis, part and parcel of which has been to warrant from the text our impression that Lance has been able to tell PE about what he wants him to hear, in his own words and in his own way; while at the same time the researcher remains accountable for how the focus of the interview has remained on the questions and interests informing the research. Riessman's (1993) and Mishler's (1994) development of Gee's (1991) model to extended stretches of jointly constructed discourse appears to offer a methodology both suitable to the kind of textual material we are working with and consonant with the various theoretical issues informing our approach.

This chapter has suggested: (i) that differing transcriptions elicit differing analyses, (ii) that the narrative section emerges through processes of joint construction and (iii) that this section is embedded or nests thematically in the surrounding text which is itself jointly constructed. By locating text interactionally, in the context of its co-construction, the pace of a process of 'backgrounding' and 'foregrounding' of themes can be discerned that feeds into and flows out of this situated stretch of embedded narrative. Mishler (1994: 3) argues that although typically research interviewers' questions and answers are 'not represented as parts of the stories themselves', they are nevertheless 'essential to interpretation of how the stories develop'. From the above analysis, it appears that in our example the researcher's core question provided an overall context of jointly elaborated enquiry in which primary themes were developed (functioning and interacting in constitutive, propositional ways) and in which personal narratives were embedded, taking up, integrating and re-contextualising further thematic developments. To the extent that this is the case, personal narrative analysis stripped of context is at risk also of being stripped of levels of 'meaning sense' (Gee, 1991: 23) that are critical both to privileging rather than appropriating the 'traces' or cues of persons' own meaning-making, and to hearing how 'culture "speaks itself" through an individual's story' (Riessman, 1993: 5).

Finally, these ideas support a provisional working definition of personal narrative arising in the interview context that is suitable to our interview material and theoretical approach. Personal narrative is (i) a respondent's personal story that comprises a relatively discrete, discursively coherent and thematically interwoven subsection of interview text which is, nevertheless, (ii) jointly constructed over the real time of the interview with the interviewer in ways that (iii) privilege the researcher's areas of interest qua research, but (iv) that privilege the respondent's views, responses, voice, experience and meaning-making, in relation to those areas of research interest.

3
Linguistic Tools and Interpretive Levels: Beginning Interpretation

Interactional processes [handwritten annotation]

Aims: to extend narrative analysis to thematic interpretation of the interview as co-construction while privileging the participant's meaning-making

In this chapter, our discussion and demonstration of narrative analysis is extended to a significantly longer stretch of Lance's interview text. Looking at longer texts facilitates their analysis in terms of interactional processes, in terms of voices in context rather than disconnected responses to disembodied questions. We focus on thematic analysis between and across research interview questions, integrating Gee's (1991) 'micro' with 'macro' linguistic building-blocks but also including the interviewer in the transcription. Here we grapple with an important methodological commitment: that, in order to privilege the participant's meaning-making, attention must be paid to how the text was said in the context of the interview. We argue that this determination to focus on how the participant construes his perceptions and experience effectively *increases* critical interpretive access to links between how he actively situates himself through personal narrative, and what canonical narratives may be employed in this. It may also suggest to what extent the canonical narrative warrants or is resisted by personal narrative, possibly in favour of contesting, potentially 'alternative, "replacement discourses", that fuel positive social constructions' (Henry and Milovanovic, 1996: x).

Broadly, our methodological argument aims to resist the decontextualisation of texts and in particular their traditional presentation as 'sole authored' which has sustained a positivist assumption of objectivity (Mishler, 1994). Instead, we see transcription and analysis as continuing processes of co-construction through which texts emerge and sense is made of them interactively. As Mishler (1995: 117) has argued, the research interview is an interactional site where 'we do not *find* stories; we *make* stories. We retell our respondents' accounts through our analytic redescriptions'. Recognising that transcription and analysis are theory driven, also demonstrates that linguistic tools for narrative analysis are neither neutral in themselves nor employed neutrally. Thus, with attention to utility or application, we will further argue that greater awareness of, or accountability for, these processes offer a useful fit with therapeutic approaches critically informed by a feminist and social constructionist perspective.

Gee *et al.* (1992: 228) distinguish between two research 'stances', one concerned with the structure of discourse 'for its own sake', the other more in relation to 'social, cognitive, political, or cultural processes and outcomes'. Often these stances inform one another. Discourse analysis, in contrast to grammatical theory, has a special interest in 'discourse genres' that, by definition, tend to be longer than single sentences (e.g. poems, descriptions, conversations of various kinds). Our analysis of research interview text exemplifies a discourse genre being looked at both in terms of discourse structure and in part as possible 'evidence' relating to psychosocial processes. Like any discourse genre, our text can be defined or approached in various ways. Gee *et al.* suggest two linguistic ways of defining texts: *etically*, that is, essentially defined by researchers for their particular purposes, and *emically*, that is, essentially defined by or in terms common to the persons being researched. The different stances serve different purposes, as Edley and Wetherell's (1997) discussion of 'top down' and 'bottom up' approaches to research suggest. Our purpose can be thought of as interrogating *etic* definitions of (here) male adolescent sexual offending from a standpoint privileging *emic* approaches. However the text is defined, it is clear that any discourse genre is produced or '*performed* within a particular context' (Edley and Wetherell, 1997: 234), whether or not context is acknowledged let alone considered. Thus, the assumption that '(a)ll thinking and all language use are social activities and, therefore, are inherently dialogic' (ibid.: 235), supports the use of a methodology capable of entering into narrative as a discursive, context-sensitive process of coproduction.

Over this and the next chapter our unit of narrative analysis will be the 145 lines of Question 3 (Q3) transcribed from PE's audio taped second research interview with Lance (L2). Whereas the focus of Lance's first interview discussed in the previous chapter was 'offence-related', this interview focuses on 'other parts' of the boy's life in order to 'get a bigger picture'. The aim of our analysis is to be illustrative and suggestive, not comprehensive. Therefore, we will approach the L2/Q3 text in three specific ways organised, as we will argue, around three demonstrable 'parts' into which it can be linguistically structured. In this chapter, we will focus on the first part. We will first briefly revisit Gee's (1991) 'micro' linguistic tools demonstrated in the previous chapter (pitch glide, idea units and lines). We will then introduce and demonstrate the 'macro' structural components of stanzas, strophes and parts, with a view, in effect, to defining the methodological meaning and means of a thematic interpretation. On this basis, in Chapter 4, we will offer as an example an extended and detailed analysis of the second part of Q3. This will pay attention to how critical narrative analysis can serve to privilege the respondent's sense-making on the one hand, while on the other, helping the researcher–interpreter to resist 'ascriptivism' by remaining alert to the co-constructive work of the linguistic cues signifying choices, performing subject positions and organising thematic developments around both personal and canonical narrative material. Turning to the third part of the extract, we will conclude Chapter 4 by carrying forward certain central themes which, because they are clearly 'cued' by the text, offer an acceptable interpretive basis for some remarks relating to constitutive canonical narratives and suggesting the importance of personal narrative material as a potential resource for therapeutic generation of possible alternative, counter-hegemonic discourses, social practices and identities.

Linguistic tools and interpretive questions: structural and interrogative constraints on meaning

Gee's (1991) method of textual analysis highlights attention to interpretive questions raised *by participants* as conversational 'cues', or context markers, to guide the interviewer/researcher towards understandings that privilege the respondent's meaning-making. In interview-based research aiming to give centrality to the voice and sense-making of the respondent, the idea of 'interpretive questions' offers a way of addressing the limits of textual interpretation which neither slides into relativism (with its risks of losing accountability) nor assumes one 'true story' that has been there all along (with its 'realist' assumption of objectivity and normative expert knowledge). Rather, because interpretation is situated and theory driven, it is recognised as 'always partial and incomplete' (Haraway, 1988). In effect, interpretation is a professional subject position accounting in terms of the negotiation of choices amongst its own available discourses or 'interpretative repertoires', which constitute 'methods for making sense' in particular contexts and amongst particular membership categories (Wetherell, 1998: 400).

While multiple answers to interpretive questions are therefore likely, Gee (1991: 16) argues that 'many answers are ruled out by the structure of the text' – the text is not, ideologically or discursively, a free-for-all. At the same time, because Gee *et al.* (1992: 232–3) consider that 'people's texts are not trivial outcomes of communicative needs', but are purposeful and replete with 'inordinately rich meaning and structure', in the balancing act between constraints on and pluralities of meaning, they declare an ethical as well as analytical preference 'to err on the side of overinterpretation'. Specifically, 'What we seek to avoid are analyses that misconstrue the discourse of any person as meaningless or impoverished'. This form of 'positive discrimination' in favour of a person's meanings and resources for meaning-making includes a commitment to meaningful interpretations of marginalised or subjugated sense-making, such as in Gee's (1991: 37) 'senseful' reading of a language sample from a 'schizophrenic' woman.

Thus, for our purposes, in analysing processes of joint construction of extended stretches of interview text, Gee's (1991) idea of 'interpretive questions' may be understood both in terms of: (i) ways in which the researcher's own questions and responses as the researcher/interviewer contextualise and structure the conversation and also thereby constrain the interviewee's responses; and (ii) how the interviewee's questions and responses, across the 'real time' of each given interview and response to each core interview question, are organised to raise their own structural pointers or 'cues' towards 'acceptable interpretations' (ibid.: 15). We will argue that Gee's idea of interpretive questions offers a way of keeping the possibilities of multiple meanings and resonance open precisely through focusing down on personal narrative meaning-making as interactionally situated. This applies both in terms of how the research interview/text itself is performed and in terms of the constitutive presence of textually anchored social discourses or canonical narratives.

Mishler (1994: 3) characterises Gee's (1991) approach to narrative analysis as 'a hierarchically-ordered set of structural components of spoken language', comprising 'micro' components of pitch glide, idea units and lines, and 'macro' components of stanzas, strophes and parts, together contributing to the generation of thematic interpretation. How do these work together to generate a multilevelled analysis in ways that both constrain and interrogate interpretation with a view to privileging the respondent's personal narrative meaning-making?

Revisiting 'micro' components: pitch glide, idea units and lines

After a 'raw' transcription of the audio taped second research interview, including all interviewer and respondent dialogue, and noting inaudibles (e.g. ??? l. 11), pauses (e.g. 6 secs, l. 9), partial utterances (e.g. '... whether it's got to do with partic, really being outnumbered...' l. 32) and speech repairs (e.g. '... a WOMA, a WOMAN'S more likely to...' l. 58), PE then returned to the audio tape with Gee's (1991) structural tools in mind. He listened to the tape over again to make a further transcription (including various corrections to some initial mishearings) of the conversation with Lance in response to one particular question, a passage referred to as L2/Q3, specifically for thematic analysis (each of the three parts of this text will be provided in full below as the narrative analysis develops). We discussed, in the preceding chapter, the importance of paying close attention to *pitch glide*, to the way in which the text was actually *said*, in order to identify *idea units* and *lines*. Through their rising and falling intonations, as well as pauses, speakers provide cues or signals for the focus of a sentence, the information each particularly wants the hearer to notice as 'new or asserted information' (Gee, 1991: 21). This focus may include more words than the emphasised information, words leading up to and away from it. What the focus is depends both on the context in which it was spoken and what is new information in that context – points, of course, which speaker, hearer and other hearers might differ over. While the literal meaning of a sentence is not changed by the focus, it may significantly affect how the sentence fits in its immediate discursive context and with the interactional context of participant and research interviewer. Gee defines an 'idea unit' as 'any sentence with one pitch glide', with the understanding that often sentences are complex and include more than one pitch glide, each signalling a different focus and thus a distinct idea unit (ibid.: 21–2). As in the preceding chapter, throughout our discussion below, words bearing the pitch glide are in CAPITALS, and idea units distinguished between slash (/) marks.

For example, the raw text of L2/Q3 at l.20 reads:

Mum and my sisters used to get what, to watch what they want on the telly, where we wait.

As it stands the literal sense of this sentence might be simply a report along the lines of 'ladies first'. If 'sisters' were emphasised and 'mum' was not, it might suggest some sibling and/or gender rivalry with the 'we' construed as brothers. If both 'mum' and 'sisters' are emphasised and 'we' includes father and son, it might suggest family organisation around gendered loyalties. If 'used to' is emphasised, it could suggest things have changed about who now waits. Hypotheses can multiply. The same line, transcribed to attend to how Lance said it in terms of pitch glide and idea units, reads:

MUM and my SISTERS used to get what,/to watch what THEY want/on the TELLY,/where WE WAIT.

This reading provides some cues for interpretation. The ambiguity between past tense 'used to' and present tense 'we wait' recedes and gendered difference becomes the foregrounded information without, however, particular inflections on 'get what' or 'want' which might suggest rivalry or dissatisfaction about waiting. Taken in its context, discussed further below, this reading fits with the preceding conversation in which PE has recycled Q3 ('What have you learned about being a boy growing up in your family?') around the contrast 'you've got SISTERS/ that have a DIFFERENT kind of EXPERIENCE of growing up, you know, in the FAMILY', and Lance has responded with an apparently axiomatic statement, 'That the WOMEN/usually GET/ what they WANT'. Thus, the sentence at l. 20 is the start of Lance's unpacking how he has 'learned' this and some of the meanings around it, meanings which pick up more on gender ambiguities than on conflict or sibling loyalties split by gender difference.

After listening for and transcribing pitch glide and the idea units, PE began to further (re)organise the text into numbered lines. Gee (1991: 22) defines a line as 'something like what would show up as a sentence in writing', revolving around a central idea that can be understood as a 'syntactically and intonationally organised' argument. Lines are integral to the stream of speech and 'sound as if they go together' (Gee *et al.*, 1992: 247). Just as sentences may contain a number of idea units, so the transcription of one sentence may be distributed across a number of lines. Lines, like pitch glide focus and idea units, signify structural components of the text *as speech*, thus also help to provide the hearer with cues for interpretation.

For example, Lance's first sentence in our L2/Q3 text reads (ll. 1–2):

I LOVE solving/other people's PROBLEMS
but I HATE/having to SOLVE my OWN.

The argument linking the two lines of this sentence turns on the unemphasised word 'but'. Whereas each line can stand on its own both syntactically and topically, the 'but' both draws and mutes attention to their contrast and their connection. Their contrast is strongly marked by the parallel pitch glides that focus l. 1 on 'LOVE' and l. 2 on 'HATE'. This contrast makes overt the polarity muted by the unemphasised 'but'. The lines are connected by the logic that polarities are linked through contrast, for example, polarities of love/hate or problems/solutions. Nevertheless, the unemphasised 'but' may suggest some ambivalence about connecting these contrasts. This possibility seems likely because of the pitch glide difference, between 'other people's' in l. 1 and 'OWN' in l. 2, which provides an interpretive cue. The pitch glide focus on 'OWN' provides the context or frame for this sentence, not 'other people'. Lance's own life is dominated by problems, the research interview itself directly stemming from this. With the focus on 'OWN', a new contrast emerges between 'LOVE solving' and 'HATE/having to SOLVE'. The kind of problem 'solving' Lance loves is rewarding, in that he implies he can do it, and at the same time it is disconnected from himself; the kind he hates both is his 'OWN' and is compelled (the pitch glide rises through 'having to' to the focus on 'SOLVE'). Thus, the sentence may contain a significant ambivalence, muted both by the unemphasised 'but' and by the parallel pitch glide foci of love/hate, an ambivalence about whether Lance would 'LOVE' to be able to solve his 'OWN' problems like he implies he is able to solve 'other people's', or whether Lance's focus on other people's problems supports a strategy to avoid or resist what 'I HATE', that is, 'having to SOLVE my OWN'. While on the surface, this sentence makes straightforward sense almost as a kind of truism, as it is actually *said* it contains cues to an ambivalence of importance both for Lance himself and, we suggest, to anyone engaged, for example, to work therapeutically with him. Does he want to change and/or is he resistant and in denial? If 'HATE' means he feels disempowered by 'having to SOLVE' problems he has not found ways of solving, how could 'LOVE' come to mean, in relation to his 'OWN' problems, the empowerment or sense of competence and social approbation arguably available from 'solving other people's PROBLEMS'?

The line, in Gee's approach, offers a unit of discourse analysis that includes attention to idea units, which each focus 'a single piece of new information', in the somewhat wider context of an 'argument' or 'central idea around which a line is syntactically and intonationally organised' (Gee, 1991: 22). Through the lens of transcription, by paying attention to how a text is actually said, idea units and lines can be seen to contribute to 'the structure of a text which cues interpretation' (ibid.: 23).

'Macro' components: stanzas, strophes and parts

Gee (1991: 23) argues that lines fall into three larger patterns that form 'the building blocks of extended pieces of discursive language'. The first of these are *stanzas*, characterised by 'a particular point of view' (Gee *et al.*, 1992: 246) or 'groups of lines with a common theme' (Mishler, 1994: 3), a change of which signifies a change of stanza. Second, stanzas tend to come in related pairs referred to as *strophes* (Gee, 1991: 23). Third, strophes in turn compose larger units called *parts*, which make up the story as a whole.

In order to illustrate and then discuss these points, we reproduce in Figure 3.1 the opening stretch of our retranscribed L2/Q3 text, including the transitional lines (ll. 1–11) from question 2 (L2/Q2) in the conversational context of which PE begins (at l. 11) to introduce Q3.

Figure 3.1   Strophes, stanzas and lines

(Transition from end Q2 links the themes of gender and problem-solving, providing a context for PE to 'move on' to Q3)

(Evaluative couplet)
  1. *L*: I LOVE solving/other people's PROBLEMS
  2. but I HATE/having to SOLVE my OWN.

Strophe 1
(Is L's evaluation gendered?)

Stanza 1
(PE frames his assumption as a question)
  3. *PE*: Uuh-huh. Yeah. Do you think THAT'S something/that's kind of CHARACTERISTIC of BOYS,
  4. you know, like to get involved in sort of SORTING OUT the other person's problems
  5. and not so much DEAL WITH, you know, LOOK/at their OWN,
  6. or is THAT something
     L: Yeah/
     PE: PARTICULAR to YOU?

Stanza 2
(L's qualified response)
  7. *L*: Um, I don't KNOW about/sorting out OTHER PEOPLE'S PROBLEMS
     PE: Yeah
  8. *L*: but it's MORE LIKELY, you know,/NOT TO BOTHER about their OWN.
  9. *PE*: Yeah.
     L: Um.
     PE: That's INTERESTING. (6 secs).

Part 1 (Q3)
(A narrative of gendered learning in L's family:
'the women usually get what they want')

Strophe 1
(Co-construction of the narrative theme)

Stanza 1
(PE constructs Q3)
  10. *PE*: Sorry, I'm just keeping an EYE/on the TIME.
  11. Need to MOVE on ??
  12. [Q3] So, thinking AGAIN about, um,

Figure 3.1   Continued

13. in terms of GROWING UP/and growing up in YOUR FAMILY/AS A BOY,
14. because you've got SISTERS/that have a DIFFERENT kind of EXPERIENCE of growing up,/you know, in the FAMILY/and the WORLD and so on, school,
15. but in terms of GROWING UP AS A BOY/in YOUR FAMILY/
16. what do you, what would you say you've LEARNED/about being a BOY/by GROWING UP in your home?

Stanza 2
(Co-constructing the possibility of the opening narrative:
L provides the focus, PE invites elaboration)

17. *L:* That the WOMEN/ usually GET/what they WANT.
18. *PE:* Uhum, so THAT'S what?
    L: Um.
    PE: Yeah
    L: Um
19. *PE:* How did you LEARN that?/
    L: I don't know, you just???
    PE: Yeah

Strophe 2
(Narrative account of learning from family experience)

Stanza 3
(Women's wants – an observation)

20. *L:* MUM and my SISTERS used to get what,/to watch what THEY want/on the TELLY,
21. where WE WAIT./If there's a GAP/we'd watch what WE WANT, you know.
22. *PE:* That would be TRUE/for your DAD as well/WOULD it?
23. *L:* YEAH, MOSTLY./If there's anything HE WANTS to watch,/it's MORE PROBABILITY that/he'll have to TAPE IT/and watch it LATER./
    PE: Right

Stanza 4
(Father's work – an explanation for waiting)

24. *L:* Even though he's, NOW,/that's NOT so RIGHT./Um, she's a, NOT because my MUM'S LETTING/him WATCH what he WANTS/
    PE: Yeah
25. *L:* but BECAUSE he's NOT home,/he's a long distance TRUCK DRIVER/
    PE: Yeah, yeah.

Stanza 5
(An embedded but uncertain conclusion)

26. *L:* Um, so at the MOMENT, you know,/at HOME/it's ME, my SISTER, my MUM/
    PE: Yeah
27. *L:* you know, I'm not SURE if it's because/I'M OUTNUMBERED,/
28. it ALWAYS SEEMS, you know, like/WHAT THEY WANT WE GET./
    PE: Yeah.

Figure 3.1 Continued

Strophe 3
(Emergence of a linked but new narrative theme)

Stanza 6
(PE reconstructs Q3)
29. And you're the YOUNGEST at HOME now/ARE you?
30. *L:* Yeah, I'm the YOUNGEST/of the FAMILY.
31. *PE:* Yeah. So how much do you think that has to do with AGE,/how much do you think it has to do with being OUTNUMBERED,/and how much do you THINK it has to do with being a BOY/growing up in the FAMILY?/

Stanza 7
(L dismantles Q3, reflects, introduces own theme)
32. *L:* (3 secs) I'm not too SURE ABOUT, you know,/whether it's got ANYTHING to do WITH partic,/REALLY being OUTNUMBERED,/um, or REALLY being a BOY, you know.
33. It's a CASE of/the WOMEN BEING,/you know, I DON'T KNOW,
34. I suppose by SAYING IT was/CONTRADICTING what I was/SAYING EARLIER. Um,
35. so in SOME CASES/WOMEN are MORE STUBBORN
    PE: Uhu
36. *L:* but in OTHER cases/THEY'RE NOT./
    PE: Yeah.

Strophe 4
(Narrative themes connect)
Stanza 8
(PE reforms Q3 around L's new theme)
37. *PE:* Can you give me an EXAMPLE,
38. like in YOUR FAMILY,/WHAT have you LEARNED about
39. when they are MORE STUBBORN/and when they're LESS STUBBORN?

Stanza 9
(Gendered wants/gendered jobs)
40. *L:* Um, they're MORE STUBBORN/in what they want to WATCH on the TELLY,/a bit LESS STUBBORN/about what they have for DINNER, or, um.
41. It's USUALLY, you know, THAT/ME or MY DAD, you know,/will be ASKED MORE OFTEN/what WE want for DINNER/than RATHER my mum just going through/and COOKING something.
42. *PE:* Right. So she'd like COOK/with YOU in MIND?
    L: Yeah.
43. *PE:* But if it's sort of TAKING LEISURE TIME/around the TV, RELAXING
    L: Um/
    PE: it would be more that THEY'D CHOOSE/what to WATCH?
    L: Yeah.

Having begun the work of retranscription in terms of pitch glide focus, idea units and lines, the use of larger components for analysis – stanzas, strophes and parts – soon becomes helpful in the overall structural organisation of longer stretches of text. Structurally speaking, the lines are first grouped into stanzas, lines organised around a particular perspective or common theme; then into strophes, stanzas (often paired but not always) that are thematically connected; and finally into parts, thematically related strophes that constitute 'sections or episodes of the overall story' (Mishler, 1994: 13). The sense of 'finding' these structures, as it were, out there in the text, needs to be tempered by a reflexive awareness that there is clearly a creative latitude in organising the lines which indicates that this structuring itself is an active and interpretive process in response to the text. As Mishler (1994: 4) states, 'unitising a stretch of speech into this set of interdependent categories is not a mechanical process but an interpretive one'.

It can be seen above that each stanza, strophe and part is labelled. These headlines emerge through, as well as guide, a circular process of analysis that begins with the analytical tools, results through closer listening and reading in new or adjusted understanding, and returns to the use of the analytical tools informed by developing interpretive responses. They thus reflect and make transparent a 'trail' of interpretive choices around the process of sense-making involved in the nitty-gritty activity of structurally organising the lines of text. They also constitute an outline of a given stretch of text that, as Gee argues, helps to show 'patterns of structure and meaning' (Gee *et al.*, 1992: 244). We have followed Mishler in extending Gee's approach by taking an interpretive interest in 'how the dynamics of the interview, the dialectic of questions and responses, produces the account we traditionally assign to the respondent' (Mishler, 1994: 11), deliberately including the interaction between the speakers by which, in real time, our text was jointly produced. Working from the premise that lines are distinguished by a central idea or argument, and that stanzas are groups of thematically related lines from 'a particular point of view' (Gee *et al.*, 1992: 246), we have chosen at various points to include changes of speaker on occasion within one line and on other occasions split the lines of one speaker's sentence across two distinct stanzas.

For the moment, focusing only structurally on how the use of Gee's 'macro' tools has transformed 'raw' text to its layout above, what can be immediately discerned by taking a closer look? Clearly, how the 'Evaluative couplet', ll. 1–2, flows out of the preceding Q2 conversation cannot be identified here; it is outside the scope of this discussion, although our headline typically suggests its linguistic function, to indicate 'the point of a story and what it is the narrator considers makes the story "tellable"' (Gee *et al.*, 1992: 248). We have suggested above in our 'micro' analysis a possible interpretation of these lines: that they serve to voice a particular dilemma for Lance. It can readily be seen that this creates a framework for PE's transition from the ending of Q2 in that, across Strophe 1, in Stanza 1 (ll. 3–6) PE poses a question, linked to the couplet by the referent 'THAT's' (l. 3), which in Stanza 2 (ll. 7–9) Lance responds to, but, as the 6-second pause (l. 9) suggests, he does not then expand on. We have therefore punctuated the conversational interface between Q2 and Q3 at ll. 10 and 11 where PE, somewhat clumsily, specifies his decision to 'MOVE on'.

The textual layout above also clearly shows that ll. 10–43 have been identified as Part 1 of Q3, structurally composed of new Strophes 1 to 4. Strophe 1 is dominated by PE's first asking of Q3 (across Stanza 1: ll. 12–16), triggering in Stanza 2 Lance's initial response (l. 17) which, followed by PE's reiteration of the theme of 'learning' (e.g. ll. 16 and 19), effectively serves as an Abstract for what we have labelled under Strophe 2 as Lance's (first Q3) 'narrative account of learning from family experience', the opening line (l. 20) of which we have considered above. This personal narrative material has been organised stanzaically to distinguish in Stanza 3 (ll. 20–3) the themes of 'Women's wants' and in Stanza 4 (ll. 24–5) 'Father's work'. Stanza 5 (ll. 26–8) is thematically coherent with Stanzas 3 and 4, but can be structurally distinguished around Lance's 'so' (l. 26) as the conclusion of a line of argument, a thematic summary, if not exactly integration, of the points of view expressed across Stanzas 3 and 4. Line 28 clearly loops back to l. 17 and reinforces as a conclusion Lance's opening 'abstract', although with some voiced uncertainty as to why (l. 27). In Strophe 3, across Stanza 6, PE offers Lance some options for further reflection on the theme of gendered learning, which, across Stanza 7, Lance first dismantles and then replaces with a new explanatory gendered theme of 'stubbornness' (l. 35).

By asking for an 'EXAMPLE' (l. 37), PE drops his own options in relation to which Strophe 3 is organised, structurally signifying new Strophe 4 narration. In Stanza 8 he carries forward Lance's theme of comparative 'CASES' (ll. 35–6) of women's stubbornness, now framed in terms of 'in YOUR FAMILY,/WHAT have you LEARNED' (l. 38), which Lance accepts and expands on in domestic detail across Stanza 9. Part 1 of Q3, this layout suggests, coheres around Lance's first thematic narrative responses to PE's first articulations of Q3. It shows PE and Lance co-constructing an initial fit between the thematically recycled framework of PE's core question and both how Lance positions himself in relation to this question as well as what accounts and practices this positioning privileges in terms of his own thematic focus and development.

Even this summary description of our Q3/Part 1 textual formatting above, achieved with the help of the 'macro' linguistic tools (stanzas, strophes and parts), demonstrates at least two important points. First, organising the text in terms of these interdependent categories is clearly an intimately and circularly interpretive activity. Second, this activity, anchored in the invitations and constraints of the text as *said*, is structurally capable of integrating the respondent as well as the interviewer into the transcript making available for analysis the co-creation of both the questions and responses constituting the linguistic flow of conversation, a point we will return to in terms of power and the co-construction of meaning. We emphasise, and have argued above, that these points are easily forgotten or dismissed in *etic* or 'top down' interpretations of texts where 'realist' objectivity is taken for granted and professional/expert knowledges typically appropriate respondents' meaning-making. Instead, we suggest that reflexive awareness of these points is a critical responsibility and methodological resource in theorising and analysing 'how narratives work and the work they do' (Mishler, 1995: 117).

Thematic interpretation

Gee (1991: 27 f) proposes five interpretive levels of structure and meaning which are conceived hierarchically – each is inclusive of those 'below' and must be taken into account by those 'above'. These levels are informed by the linguistic tools (idea units, lines, stanzas, strophes and parts), each of which, by contributing its own kind of interpretive cues and questions, helps to ground the overall thematic interpretation of textual meanings in and through linguistic structures. We take it that these interpretive levels are not necessarily developed in a linear or consecutive manner, but mutually and recursively inform one another across the systematic listening/reading and re-listening/re-reading of a text. Below, we outline these levels, making further illustrative use of Lance's L2/Q3, Part 1 text.

Level 1 is, in effect, the text as re-transcribed along the lines demonstrated and discussed above. A critical interpretive question raised at this level is: *How has this text been organised or structured in order to convey its meanings?* We have suggested how the processes of our Part 1 transcription drew attention to certain meanings and how those meanings also affected to some extent our construction/interpretation of the text's structure. In particular, we introduced 'the dialectic of questions and responses' (Mishler, 1994: 11) into transcription. One reason for this has been to show that Lance's responses cannot legitimately be read as snippets isolated from the interview context; furthermore, PE's own questioning and responses are also contextually constructed. While the flow of the semistructured interview is largely PE's responsibility and initiated by him, it is not unidirectional (question–answer), but involves a mutual negotiation of meanings, of questions as well as trajectories of responses, in the co-production of the conversation. This activity has demonstrable bearing on analysis of the distribution of discursive power evident, for example, in how we have structured Part 1 of our L2/Q3 text in Figure 3.1.

Looking at our organisation of the Q2/Q3 interface (ll. 1–11), PE, with the passing of interview time in mind, states a gender assumption in the form of a question (ll. 3–5), in part because he is curious whether Lance's preceding evaluative couplet (ll. 1–2) is gendered in his own thinking, and also because this frame moves the interview on in the direction of Q3 which is designed to raise conversation around gendered learning and family experience. In the real time of the interview, PE's question does not pick up on the particular ambivalence suggested/noticed retrospectively in our analysis of the evaluative couplet, although he does invite Lance to respond either in terms of what he considers 'CHARACTERISTIC of BOYS' (l. 3) or in terms 'PARTICULAR to YOU' (l. 6). Lance's response, structurally signified as Stanza 2, starts with a disclaimer – 'Um, I don't KNOW about'

(l. 7) – directed at and adjusting the invitation to comment on whether he thinks it is 'CHARACTERISTIC of BOYS' 'to get involved in sort of SORTING OUT the other person's problems'. This part of PE's question links with Lance's comment in l. 1, 'I LOVE solving other people's PROBLEMS'. Lance did not want to say whether it was characteristic of boys, generally, to be sorting out other people's problems, although he suggested that he himself loved doing it. Thus, this disclaimer prevents his comment from becoming a general evaluation about boys and at the same time reinforces that his statement, 'I LOVE solving other people's PROBLEMS', is, in PE's words, 'PARTICULAR to YOU'. However, ll. 7 and 8 are linked (like ll. 1 and 2) by an unemphasised 'but' on a rising pitch glide to 'MORE LIKELY'. The focus shift from 'don't KNOW' to 'MORE LIKELY' returns Lance's response to the gender frame PE has put around his evaluative couplet. This leads to the generalisation that in his view what is 'CHARACTERISTIC of BOYS' is 'NOT TO BOTHER about their OWN' ('PROBLEMS').

If the text raises the question of why Lance makes this distinction, one acceptable reading of it could be this: an interest in solving other people's problems is 'PARTICULAR' to Lance, whereas not bothering about his 'OWN' is typical of 'BOYS'. Both of these positions in relation to PE's question may enable Lance to see or show himself in a culturally normative light if we understand helping others to be a normal good and not liking to solve (disconnecting from) their own problems as normal for boys. After PE's rather lame response, 'That's INTERESTING' (l. 9), followed by an awkward 6-second silence (l. 10), he offers an apology explaining what has probably been obvious to Lance, that he is watching the clock which means, in this context, 'Need to MOVE on' (l. 11). We have discussed our transitional layout of these lines, which indicates structurally that both Lance and PE have negotiated a so far unspoken/unclear ending to Q2 – on *this* side of the pause there is no more to say, or at least no more interviewer permission to say more, on *that* side of the pause something connected yet also new may begin.

What we want to highlight illustratively here in relation to the Level 1 contribution to thematic interpretation, is that, just as PE's question is constructed in relation to his own assumptions, so Lance's response is an *account of himself* linked or situated in relation both to the constraints of PE's question and also constructing meanings of great importance to himself as a boy who is being interviewed precisely because his sexual offending is not considered good or normal. Clearly, PE's questions and responses implicitly depend on and reinforce an assumed power differential between Lance, who has contracted to be interviewed, and himself as the researcher/interviewer who, with his questions literally to hand on a typed piece of paper, will control through the semistructured interview schedule the core thematic transitions of the interview. At the same time, however, Lance's contribution to the development of PE's question (ll. 3–6) is significant and critical. Adjusting the frame of this question from either/or to both/and, Lance constructs a view of himself in which loving to solve other people's problems is 'particular' to him while hating to solve his own problems is 'characteristic of boys'; he thus positions himself discursively as both a good and a typical boy. In this sense there is an important interactional parity between respondent and interviewer: just as Lance's *account* or responses can be seen to be interactionally accomplished, so PE's *questioning* can be seen to be interactionally produced, including, as he does 'MOVE on', his on-line transitional articulations of Q3. While an underemphasis on interviewer power fails to be reflexive and to recognise related difficulties for instance of appropriation, an overemphasis can also misconstrue the significant power of respondents in what they contribute to and how they participate in the process of co-constructing the interview, how they position themselves as well as the interlocutor through and in relation to their unfolding personal narrative material.

Level 2 is concerned with the ways in which language practices are used to create cohesion within lines, between lines, across stanzas and over the whole text. This level raises interpretive questions about: *Why has the speaker (or, have the speakers) made this particular kind of connection at this point?* and *How does this connection make sense within the logic of particular narrative parts and of the overall jointly produced interview?*

For example, in the Q3/Part 1 text above, we have commented on Lance's use of the unemphasised 'but' connecting ll. 1 and 2, as well as ll. 7 and 8, and possible themes this suggests. We have noticed PE's use of the referent 'THAT'S' (l. 3) which carries forward possible meanings from Lance's 'evaluative couplet' while raising the linking theme of gender central to Q3. We argued that through his qualified

response to PE's question (ll. 3–6), Lance (ll. 7–8) constructs a normative story for himself as a boy connected with an ambivalence in
the couplet that is very central to his current situation – does he or
does he not want to solve the problem of his sexual offending? But
an even more fundamental question nests within this one: how can
Lance learn to be as effective 'to SOLVE my OWN' (l. 2) problems as
he suggests he is at solving 'other people's'? We have suggested that
this question of learning is then carried forward and developed
across Q3 as a central theme that is intimately and overtly gendered.
Thus, through syntactical cohesion across the Q2/Q3 transitional
Stanzas (ll. 1–9), meanings are carried forward, modified and negotiated, to create a context for Q3 in which Lance's meaningful
responses to PE's core question – '…what would you say you've
LEARNED/about being a BOY/by GROWING UP in your home?'
(l. 16) – continue to develop accounts of gendered learning that will
have direct bearing on the theme of gendered problem solving (later
developed across Part 2 of Q3).

Other language practices creating and generating cohesion across
Q3/Part 1 can also be seen. PE's first articulation of Q3 (ll. 12–16)
demonstrates both his own choices around sense-making and preferred connections, and initiates certain context markers in relation
to which he invites Lance to develop a further trajectory of personal
narrative connections. In terms of sense and delivery, PE could simply have skipped straight to l. 16. In the context of the conversation,
however, the positioning of Q3 at this point is crucial in that PE
wants both to maintain links with what has come before, thus valuing what Lance has already been saying, and to mark what is different about this next core question. Gee *et al.* (1992: 283), privileging
the meaningfulness of peoples' speaking, observe that:

> false starts and repairs are meaningful indications of underlying
> planning, and so themselves are also guides to structure and
> meaning…. People tend to display such speech disruptions when
> they are planning a new or major division in their text 'on-line',
> as they are speaking.

In this sense, a 'disruption' may serve as a cue to structural continuity or cohesion. While we will notice such on-line disruptions in
Lance's discourse, here PE can be seen to negotiate his entry into Q3
with a false start at ll. 12–13 – 'thinking AGAIN about, um,/in terms

of GROWING UP/and growing up in YOUR FAMILY/AS A BOY' – which indicates a tactical correction. While 'AGAIN' fits with Q1 and Q2 in the broad second interview terms of 'growing up into a young man', PE realises, in the speaking (somewhere around the 'um') that it does not fit with his intended focal emphasis in Q3 on 'growing up in YOUR FAMILY'. Similarly, the sense of l. 14, which strongly marks gender difference through PE's pitch glide emphasis on SISTER, DIF-FERENT, EXPERIENCE, is integrated into his repositioned emphasis in l. 15: here he virtually repeats the content of l. 13, but with a shift to 'AS A BOY/in YOUR FAMILY' which inflects and privileges his pre-ferred context of asserted gender difference. Finally, in this articula-tion of Q3, PE proposes a further frame for discursive coherence by projecting a virtual outline of categories for reflecting on gender difference: EXPERIENCE, FAMILY, WORLD (and its add-on subcate-gory of 'school' which, in fact, emerges as a central thematic and gendered context Lance chooses to develop in Q3/Part 3). Attention to Level 2 sense-making serves to keep interpretive practices alert to and anchored in the linguistic structures through which coherent patterns or themes emerge and develop.

Level 3 involves 'distinguishing the *main line* of the plot from material *off the main line*' (Gee, 1991: 29). Gee puts the question raised by this level of interpretation as: *'What's the main point or sig-nificance of this plot?'* or, in short, *'So what?'* In discussing above our macro-structuring of Q3/Part 1, we suggested that l. 17 – 'That the WOMEN/usually GET/what they WANT' – serves as an abstract for Strophe 2, Lance's first Q3 narrative account of learning from family experience. We explained our stanzaic organisation with related headlines across this stretch of text, the last line of which emphati-cally reasserts and adjusts the abstract – 'WHAT THEY WANT WE GET' (l. 28). Two examples of *main line* and *off the main line* of the plot can be discerned here, the first in relation to Lance's linguistic activity, the second in relation to PE's. *First*, between his abstract at l. 17 and his conclusion at l. 28, Lance's narrative unfolds in ways which shift the main point or significance of the plot from the more axiomatic, generalising tone of l. 17 to an articulation at l. 28 now enriched with intimate family details about 'TELLY' watching and employment arrangements, elaborated and explained with special and discerning attention to gendered domestic status. As an account of his learning (l. 19), this Strophe 2 narrative represents an interactional activity in which, as narrator, Lance is positioning himself through language in relation to his own experience of women in his family and in relation to the interview process itself. He is fitting his means of expression simultaneously to a story of his experience and to the frames of reference/questioning of the listener. In this activity how the story is narrated is part and parcel not simply of what it is about but what it is being told for, its 'main point'. What begins as a story to illustrate an apparently axiomatic statement becomes a gendered activity of positioning himself in relation both to 'MUM and my SISTERS' as well as his 'DAD'. *Second*, a measure of Lance's emotional and narrative investment in the assertion of this as the main line of his 'plot', can be seen in how he deftly discards as off the main line both his own tentative explanation (l. 28) and then dismantles PE's suggestions (l. 31, e.g. of 'AGE', 'being OUTNUMBERED', or 'being a BOY'), replacing these with the gendered thematic explanation of stubbornness (ll. 35–6).

Finally, attention to main line plot does not discount the importance of 'off main line' material. For instance, it can be argued that the shift we have suggested above from axiomatic statement (l. 17) through personal narrative (l. 28), also prefigures through 'family', and serves as a cultural training ground for, exactly the reproduction and dominance of this kind of gendered canonical 'truism'. While this discussion could be legitimately considered in interpreting this text, we suggest that in context discerning Lance's main line plot serves to privilege both how his narrative works and, at this point, the work to which he is putting it. At this point, the narrative text (Strophe 2) warrants neither interpretation of resistance to, nor reproduction of, its canonical abstract, although it does show Lance actively positioning both himself and PE in relation to an experience of gendered learning in his family.

Level 4 concerns the subject positions or points of view from which the material in a stanza is viewed. Gee (1991: 30) states that, grammatically, the 'psychological subject' of a point of view can, with some exceptions, be identified by 'the grammatical subject of a main clause', whether on or off the main line of the plot (*Level 3*). Identifying the psychological subjects of stanzas across a stretch of text helps to raise interpretive questions that may only be answerable in terms of the most inclusive interpretive level of narrative meaning and structure. These questions concern not only, *Who or what is the subject of a given stanza?* but also, *Why does a narrator change psycho-logical subjects or shift points of view and are there patterns in these changes?* This interpersonal activity might be considered in terms of subject positioning performed to accomplish shifting discursive selves as well as in terms indicative of dominant discourses affecting the 'subjection' of an individual, of canonical narratives constraining choices of possible identities. That is, questions of 'point of view' reveal how the speaker can be both a 'narrative agent' and 'subject to' powerful discursive structures.

In order to give a flavour of how this kind of micro-reading can contribute to narrative analysis, we revisit the opening stretch of illustrative text discussed above (Figure 3.1, ll. 1–28). In the transition to and first asking of Q3, PE maintains a focus on the grammatical subject 'you' (e.g. ll. 3, 16, 19). This is consistent with his declared research interests in the boy's 'own words' and 'own points of view'. Lance, on the other hand, shifts psychological subjects in ways that raise significant interpretive questions. For instance, in ll. 1, 2, 7, 27 'I'/'I'm' is the subject. Between ll. 7 and 27, as Lance develops his opening narrative in Part 1, psychological subjects can be seen to shift around gender identities: female – l. 17 'WOMEN', l. 20 'MUM...SISTERS', l. 24 'she's'; male – l. 21 'we'd' (Lance and his father), l. 24 'he's'. Lance's first shift to 'WOMEN' in Stanza 2 (l. 17) is carried through the whole of Strophe 2, being central to Stanzas 3 and 4, with a return to 'I'm' in l. 27 Stanza 5. What meanings does this shifting around gender suggest and how do these meanings fit with Lance's shift to 'I'm'? Such questions have implications for any acceptable interpretation that might be considered, needing to be answered in ways that *both* fit the points of view of the psychological subjects of each stanza, *and* fit with the broader interpretive structure and meaning of this stretch of text. The psychological subject 'WOMEN' (l. 17), carried from Stanza 2 into Strophe 2, is here contextualised by family, Lance's prototypical/representative women, 'MUM and my SISTERS' (l. 20): the general has become particular, gender has become people and practices in relationships in his experience. However, why does Lance shift from 'we' at l. 21 to the grammatical subject of l. 23 which appears to be a kind of impersonal 'it's' (as can also be seen in Stanza 2, l. 8)? One way of understanding this is that whereas the women are actively constructed, men in the family (in the person of Lance's father) are at risk of being construed as passive, literally organised, for example, more by 'PROBABILITY' than by choice or presence. While the literal meaning of Lance's narrative seems clear at one level, perhaps (over)hearing himself telling it in the interview context of a male listener begins to create some narrative difficulties, which the transition to Stanza 4 suggests.

After wondering here if there was any grammatical subject, we suggest there are two (indicated by underlining):

24. *L*: Even though <u>he's</u>, NOW,/that's NOT so RIGHT./Um, <u>she's</u> a, NOT because my MUM'S LETTING/him WATCH what he WANTS/
    PE: Yeah
25. *L*: but BECAUSE he's NOT home,/he's a long distance TRUCK DRIVER/
    PE: Yeah, yeah.

In l. 24 both 'he's' and 'she's' are grammatical subjects. However, 'he's' is part of a false start during which, in the course of his flow of speech, Lance seems to reflect on something he intended to say: the pitch glide focus on 'NOW,/that's NOT so RIGHT' suggests a current evaluative process on the basis of which he chooses to change viewpoint to 'she's', and the stanza develops in terms of his mother as psychological subject. From this point of view, the initial grammatical subject, 'he's', Lance's father, becomes the subordinate clause of l. 25. Why does Lance shift point of view this way? Interpretations of this stanza are constrained to some extent by needing to respond to this question both in terms of the stanza itself and the more inclusive levels of narrative structure and meaning. We suggest that Lance's shift of psychological subjects here may indicate that what he has just said about how and when he and his father 'watch what we WANT' (l. 21) is not what he is evaluating. His shift to 'she's' involves him in a difficult explanation of complexities of gendered parental power arrangements. The difficulty may be suggested by Lance's second false start – 'Um, she's a' (l. 24) – before he finds his line of narration. His explanation is addressed both to PE as male listener, and to himself as narrator aiming for (an air of) veracity as he articulates and positions himself in relation to his experience as he wants PE to understand it. The shift of psychological subjects enables Lance to address overtly the possibly implicit and apparently worrying suggestion of an imbalance of power in his use of the 'TELLY' to illustrate 'That the WOMEN/usually GET/what they WANT'. He is able to exonerate his mother from both a female pre-rogative to choose for herself and a position of controlling his father – for example, 'NOT because my MUM'S LETTING/him WATCH what he WANTS' (l. 24) – by clarifying that television-watching arrangements are a domestic accommodation to his father's world of work. That the women get to watch what they want could almost literally demonstrate that his father is 'in the driving seat' 'BECAUSE he's NOT home,/he's a long distance TRUCK DRIVER' (l. 25). But does it? This reading retains an important ambiguity: does Stanza 4 do more to exonerate his mother from, or elevate his father to a controlling position? In effect, the grammatical subordination of 'he's' fits more with the impact of his father's *absence* on family organisation than his active presence. The shift of psychological sub-ject to his mother may fit more with an uncertainty of Lance's own about his mother's power (maybe resolved for his father by not being much at home, but not for Lance who still lives at home), and less with some assumed case for patriarchy.

The structural shift to Stanza 5, we suggest, is signified precisely by Lance's uncertainty about how to situate himself 'at HOME', that is, with 'my SISTERS' and 'my MUM' (l. 26), in terms of what he may want in a world of gendered experience where 'the WOMEN/usually GET/what they WANT'. In the course of Stanzas 3 and 4 'we' in 'what WE WANT' in effect becomes his father's wants with which Lance identifies along gender lines but in relation to which as a child/boy his own wants were not distinguished; significantly, Lance as psy-chological subject only reappears in Stanza 5, 'I'm' (l. 27). As he draws this particular narrative section (Strophe 2) to a close, he emphasises the cohesion of his conclusion (Stanza 5) with the con-nector 'Um, so' (l. 26), but he also signifies a change of psychologi-cal subject and thematic perspective *from* others *to* himself, from his perception of how they are situated to a preoccupying uncertainty about how he and his wants are situated in relation to them – '... you know, I'm not SURE if...' (ll. 27–8). Thus, across this illustrative stretch of Part 1 text, close attention to changes of psychological sub-ject can be seen to contribute to anchoring interpretive thematic reading in distinctive language practices attuned both to the *who* and *why* of shifting perspectives and discursive positions.

Level 5, hierarchically the most inclusive interpretive level, is firmly anchored in how the smallest unit of analysis, pitch glide, signals the focus of an idea unit. In the text each focus appears in capitals, representing information the speaker is asserting as most important, relevant or new in that context. Gee (1991: 33) argues that, within and across the stanzas of a text, this focused material provides the 'images or themes out of which we are invited to build an overall interpretation of the narrative'. The focused material repeatedly raises the question: *Why is this so important?* Responses to this question constrain readings of the text in that themes emerging from the emphasised material at one level need to be taken into account at more inclusive levels of interpretation. Level 5 represents 'a "reading" of the focused material (viewed as key images or themes) within the overall structure of the narrative' which Gee refers to as '*thematic interpretation*' (ibid.).

As we have argued above, we understand the structural and interpretive uses of Gee's model of narrative analysis, amplified to encompass the research interview as discourse, to be flexible, recursive and interactive, and this is evident from our examples above. For instance, we have drawn on pitch glide cues typical of *Level 1* as part of our illustrative discussion of *Level 4* psychological subjects above. Paying close attention to focused material across Q3/Part 1 has suggested that, while Lance engages with PE's Q3 research theme of gendered learning in his family, he does so in ways that privilege not only his own perspectives but also perspectives on perspectives, both his own and PE's, and even perhaps more axiomatic/canonical ones as well. In particular, Lance's first Q3 narrative account across Strophe 2 centralises thematic reflection on why 'it ALWAYS SEEMS, you know, like/WHAT THEY WANT WE GET' (l. 28); this, in turn, finds its narrative direction, across Strophe 3, in Lance's observation that 'in SOME CASES/WOMEN are MORE STUBBORN...but in OTHER cases/THEY'RE NOT' (ll. 35–6). It is evident in Strophe 4, which we do not address here in any detail, that the theme of 'MORE STUBBORN...LESS STUBBORN' (l. 39) is carried forward and reiterates the themes of gendered wants and gendered jobs. Importantly, however, the pitch glide emphasis in Stanza 9 on 'USUALLY' (l. 41) recalibrates Lance's Stanza 4 analysis of domestic power arrangements in that exoneration is absent and instead his mother is viewed uncritically as characteristically stubborn. In the context of the conversation, this view seems to 'REALLY' (l. 32) represent a more satisfactory explanation, a more acceptable subject position, in terms of what Lance has been telling PE he has 'learned as a boy growing up in your family'. Across ll. 42–3, PE checks out and Lance confirms that he has understood correctly (enough) at this point, thus signalling, as our structural analysis shows, a conclusion of Part 1 and transition to Part 2 of Q3.

In light of these ideas, the gendered world of work, bisected between 'at HOME' and 'NOT home', provides a context in which to consider, as Seidler (1994: 118) puts it, that

> sense of the crucial tension between an individual's growing realisation of what he or she wants for themselves and the definitions that are provided for them by social relationships.

Practising to situate himself in relation to his mother and his father and their differing wants brings Lance face to face with the gendered world of work at home. As a child Lance experiences certain discourses and available definitions of himself in his relationships with his parents, his mother's presence, his father's absence. Whether, in his family, Lance sees the impact of his father's work organising gendered arrangements for 'TELLY' watching, or whether he understands this more in terms of his mother's stubbornness, is affected by how he negotiates his sense of himself and of his connections and emotional relationships with others. Our reading of Q3/Part 1 suggests there are tensions for Lance in these relationships and that his narrative material in part represents a performative, discursive activity for situating himself in relation to these relationships. In the context of situating his learning as a boy in his family principally in relation to his mother as prototypical Woman, he seems first to need to exonerate her from having power over his father, but then seems more satisfied with the explanation of her having power in the form of being 'stubborn'. The exoneration hinges on the status of his father's absence from home through work; but this status dissolves or at least becomes highly tenuous when the power of domestic arrangements is located in his mother; furthermore, the son's privileges of identifying with his father's status are inconclusive since Lance at home is still a child.

The development of Lance's narrative in effect from one of exonerating his mother from having too much power to accepting a significant way in which she personally practices power suggests that, while some ambivalence still pertains, Lance is actively engaged in *not* supporting a family or a cultural discourse in which his father's absence at work constitutes his domestic status. If, as Connell (1995: 44) argues, 'masculinities are configurations of practice structured by gender relations', then how Lance negotiates the sense of himself and his wants in relation to 'the division of social labour' as he meets it in his family relationships is a significant site in terms of his own 'emotional development'. In the following chapter, as we move on to the second part of our L2/Q3 text, we will argue that Lance's emotional development, understood in terms of emotional attachments he elaborates on during this stretch of the interview, continues to be strongly linked to the themes of gendered learning in the family and the gendered world of work. It is also connected with problematic practices that reflect his ambivalence about, and perhaps his resistance to, hegemonic gendered social narratives available for making sense of himself and of his wants, and for situating himself in relation to others.

Balancing analytical means and conceptual frameworks in the critical practice of narrative interpretations

We have used Q3/Part 1 to illustrate our understanding and application of Gee's model of narrative analysis. We have described and offered examples of how the ways in which a text is *said* can provide 'micro' and 'macro' cues raising interpretive questions that help to privilege speakers' sense-making. We have illustrated a multilevel conceptual hierarchy characterised by a number of increasingly inclusive interpretive questions, summarised in Table 3.1.

This approach is anchored in the theoretical understanding that discourse genres are socially situated and socially constituted (Gee *et al.*, 1992). It therefore argues for an interpretive reading of texts that is sensitive to wider social contexts, organising discourses and canonical narratives, as well as to the spoken linguistic co-construction of texts. This approach to extended stretches of interview text, both *invites* attention to wider social contexts and constitutive discourses, and *constrains* the ways in which these can be used as interpretive lenses for reading narrative texts. We argue that the constitutive presence, for instance, of ideological or canonical material in an

Table 3.1 Five structural levels of narrative interpretation

Level	Characteristics	Interpretive questions raised
1	Organisation of text	How has this text been organised as speech?
2	Syntax and cohesion	Why has (have) the speaker(s) made this particular connection at this point? How does this connection make sense within the logic of particular narrative sections and of the overall, jointly produced interview?
3	Mainline/off-main-line plot	What is the main point or significance of this plot? So what?
4	Psychological subjects	Who or what is the psychological subject of this stanza? Why does the narrator change subjects or shift positions/points of view? Are there patterns in these changes?
5	Focusing system	Why is this focus so important? How does it fit with other focused material?

interview must be interpreted from and in light of emphasised or focused material evident from how the text was said. Analysis of the 'inordinately rich meaning and structure' (Gee *et al.*, 1992: 232) of personal narratives in light, for example, of interpretive systems derived from professional assumptions, imported from research or clinical paradigms or particular ideological commitments, is not sufficient and could constitute implicit if not explicit appropriation. Rather, sense-making must be seen to emerge from focused material across the levels of textual interpretation in order to become acceptable and meaningful at the most inclusive level of *thematic interpretation*, where, indeed, we may hear how 'culture "speaks itself" through the individual's story' (Riessman, 1993: 5).

This balance, we suggest, is particularly important in relation to interpretive readings of texts typically subjected to expert knowledges and interpretive frameworks, moral/political as well as clinical. Both of these wider systems frameworks can be used to 'misconstrue the discourse of [participants] as meaningless or impoverished'

(Gee *et al.*, 1992: 233): the one because nothing they say is legitimate until they are properly re-socialised, the other because how they have been socialised is the object of deconstruction and delegitimisation. In Chapter 4, further developing our detailed thematic interpretation of L2/Q3, we will seek to demonstrate and maintain this balance between using analytical tools for reading the text in terms of how it was *said* and using conceptual tools for interpreting the co-construction of thematic meanings across a stretch of interview.

4
Building a Rabbit Run: Doing Thematic Interpretation

Aims: warranting interpretation from the 'trace in the talk'

In the preceding chapter we discussed and illustrated ways in which micro and macro (re)structuring of our text began at a number of levels to generate closely warranted thematic interpretation. We have argued that this approach positions us to critically address the methodological problem of 'ascriptivism', that 'tendency to impute the presence of a discourse to a piece of text without explaining the basis for specific claims' (Widdicombe, 1995: 111). While this approach to the complexities and ambiguities of texts, we suggest, respects and draws attention to 'the remarkable subtleness and sophistication of ordinary people's talk and its designed features' (Edley and Wetherell, 1997: 205), it does so not automatically but based on an ethical determination to privilege respondents' meaning-making and a practical willingness to engage at close quarters with the interactional and discursive 'messiness' of narrative co-construction. It is, therefore, worth acknowledging that this kind of intimate and extended textual analysis can be difficult to persist with: as will be evident below, close readings of this kind are laborious and complex, focusing on the fine mesh of often contradictory and fragmentary linguistic detail out of which genuine spoken narratives are made. The difficulty of carrying out and reading such detailed analytic work may in part explain (a) why snippets are typically such an attractive unit of analysis, and (b) why frequently texts simply have imposed on them conceptually coherent but imported (i.e. preordained) professional frameworks or assumptions. By contrast, in carrying forward our detailed and extended 'bottom up' thematic interpretation, we aim to illustrate how our approach can help to resist the invitations of 'ascriptivism'. We demonstrate instead, not only the co-construction of researcher/respondent concerns, but more importantly how any interpretive warrant for these must be evident first in terms of our respondent's own 'concern within the interaction and present as a trace in the talk before it can be imported into the analysis' (Edley and Wetherell, 1997: 205). Our strophe-by-strophe approach should make referencing the text relatively easy while at the same time making clear how stanzaic coherence is contextually situated and thematically developed. Our more general aim is to show, through the relentless detail of our approach, how critical narrative analysis can be applied to the complexity of a person's speech, deriving from it not a specious 'order' or 'coherence', but a sense of the struggle amongst mixed intentions, understandings and feelings, which is actually characteristic of what people do in talk with one another.

A narrative of gendered learning and identity – doing thematic interpretation

In Figure 4.1 we reproduce, and will then systematically discuss, Part 2 of Lance's Q3 text.

Figure 4.1   A narrative of gendered learning

Part 2   (A narrative of gendered learning and identity)
Strophe 5
(Co-constructing a new narrative direction)
Stanza 10
(PE recycles Q3 around contrast with L's sisters)
44. *PE*: So WHAT OTHER THINGS/have you LEARNED/about being a BOY?/That's ONE kind of thing/you've LEARNED in your family.
45. *PE*: So, what OTHER things/have you LEARNED/about being a BOY/GROWING UP in YOUR family?
46. You know, they might be DIFFERENT from what,/what your SISTERS have learned/growing up as GIRLS. (3 secs)

Stanza 11
(School and work – gendered pathways)
47. *L*: Don't know. Like, my SISTERS were/PUSHED HARDER to go/through the SCHOOL YEARS,

Figure 4.1 Continued

48. you know, where ME and my BROTHER WEREN'T.
49. It was a CASE OF, if,/if they WANT TO do the WORK/they'll DO IT,/IF they DON'T/they WON'T./
    PE: Uhum.
50. *L*: Whereas, WITH my SISTERS,/it was a case of, YOU KNOW,
51. 'You NEED TO DO THIS WORK/to get THROUGH and/to GET what you WANT', (2 sec) um (3 sec)

Strophe 6
(L reflects on a 'canonical' rumour)
Stanza 12
(L states and evaluates the rumour)
52. *PE*: So WHAT does THAT mean/about being a BOY, then,/if you DO that?
53. *L*: I don't know. (2 secs) You know, WOMEN AREN'T/SUPPOSED/to BE mo,
54. YOU KNOW/there's this THING GOING ROUND that/MEN are supposed to be MORE CLEVER
    PE: Uhuh
    L: Yeah,
55. um, which is NOT ACTUALLY TRUE.
56. Just as CLEVER (better?)/as what WOMEN are.
57. *PE*: So you've learned, have you LEARNED THAT in your family,/the idea that WOMEN/are MORE CLEVER than/MEN THINK they are?
    L: Yeah.

Stanza 13
('Consequences': L links his re-evaluation of female cleverness and his own (male) behaviour – 'offending ... anything')
58. *L*: (1 secs) Um (5 secs) a WOMA, a WOMAN'S more likely to/ THINK THINGS OUT,
59. whereas I'm ALWAYS/being TOLD, you know,/not, I HAVEN'T thought of the/ CONSEQUENCES of DOING something
    PE: Right
    L: um,
60. NOT PARTICULARLY the OFFENDING, but,/you know, ANYTHING.
    PE: Uhum
    L: Um (2 secs)
61. *PE*: So like, WHAT/
    L: Well
    PE: Yeah, SORRY/

Strophe 7
(The rabbit run – a narrative of gendered learning in L's family)
Stanza 14
(Contrasting approaches – 'a woman ... my mum'/'My dad and me')
62. *L*: Well, a WOMAN, you know,/well, SAY MY MUM
    PE: Uhum

Figure 4.1   Continued

63. *L*: SHE'S more LIKELY/to PLAN something OUT
    PE: Yeah
    L: yeah,
64. where MY DAD and ME/it's, you know, HANDS ON,/want to GET IN
    there/DOING SOMETHING.
    PE: Yeah

Stanza 15
(A personal narrative elaborating the contrast and embedding L's re-evaluation of
the 'canonical' rumour)
65. *L*: Um, like, for INSTANCE,/MAKING a RUN/which was JUST for our RABBIT,
    yeah.
66. For ME and my DAD,/we would PLAN TO GO DOWN,/just GO DOWN into the
    SHOPS,
    PE: Yeah
    L: Texas,/BUY the WOOD/for the CAGE,/BRING it back and/just MAKE IT
    PE: Yeah
    L: Yeah,
67. where my MUM was there, you know,/PEN OUT/DRAWING all these LITTLE
    SKETCHES of it,/and COUNTING OUT THE LENGTHS of WOOD/we would
    NEED/and how
    PE: Yeah
    L: MUCH it would COST.
(Evaluative coda)
68. (2 secs) Don't know. (2 secs) Um (2 secs), so WOMEN THINK MORE.
    PE: Uhum/
    L: They PLAN MORE.

Strophe 8
(Co-constructing further reflection on the gendered theme of cleverness)
Stanza 16
(L wants to be 'clever' like 'a woman … my mum')
69. *PE*: HOW do you THINK THAT'S, that's/affected YOUR VIEW/of the kind of
    BOY, YOUNG MAN,/YOU want to BECOME?
70. *L*: Don't know, um, I ALWAYS/WANTED TO BE able to
71. PLAN things out actually/det, like GOOD DETAIL
    PE: Uhum
72. *L*: um, but, you KNOW, WHATEVER HAPPENS,/you know,

Stanza 17
(The choice of mentors)
73. if I was, like, TAKE,/ONCE you were/PLANNING OUT/MAKING SOMETHING
    PE: Uhum
74. *L*: if I was to HAND it IN,
75. for SOME reason,/I'd ALWAYS CHECK IT with my MUM FIRST, you
    know,/LET HER READ THROUGH IT
    PE: Yeah

Figure 4.1 Continued

76. *L*: yeah, NOT my DAD,/LET my MUM READ THROUGH IT.
    PE: Right.

<u>Stanza 18</u>
(<u>Evaluative coda – formulation of a developmental dilemma: ambivalence of cross-</u>
<u>gender admiration</u>)

77. *L*: Um, I don't know, like WHETHER it's BECAUSE/SHE would have
    THOUGHT MORE ABOUT IT
    PE: Um

78. *L*: or WHETHER it's because/WOMEN ARE SUPPOSED to be/'the LESS
    CLEVER TYPE',/

79. so to SEE IF SHE could FOLLOW the INSTRUCTIONS, I don't know.
    PE: Uhu.

80. *L*: But, MIND you,/I WOULDN'T say mum's STUPID./
    PE: You WOULDN'T say she's stupid?/
    L: No.

We suggested earlier that the headlines resulting from transcription help to make transparent a 'trail' of inevitably interpretive choices. Before turning to a detailed strophe-by-strophe analysis of the Figure 4.1 text, Table 4.1 summarises the headlines for both Part 1 (analysed in the previous chapter) and Part 2 of L2/Q3. Although this 'outline' arises out of the more detailed analysis presented below, we include it here so that the overall shape of the narrative work can be tracked.

Our interpretive engagement with Part 2 develops across 36 lines organised into 4 Strophes and 9 Stanzas. It is evident from this outline that the Q3 research theme of 'gendered learning' in the family is carried forward from Part 1 into Part 2, across Stanza 10 where PE recycles Q3. We will suggest that through personal narratives introduced and elaborated by Lance, he can be seen to actively negotiate particular versions of this core question, and to discursively situate both PE and himself in relation to it. We will show that, though distinguishable, these narratives are also connected to one another as coherent parts of Lance's response to the constraints and opportunities offered by the overall discourse theme represented by Q3.

In Part 1, Lance introduces and develops the gendered themes of wants and stubbornness with particular reference to his parents, especially his mother. In Part 2, Lance first develops a narrative around contrasting experiences of his parents' views of schooling for their sons and daughters (Stanza 11). Out of this highly specific narrative, across Strophe 6, Lance raises a broad social narrative or *rumour* concerning the relative cleverness of men and women about

Table 4.1 Outline of the narrative text L2/Q3 – Parts 1 and 2

Transition into Q3

Q2 (end)
Lines 1–9 – PE links the themes of gender and problem-solving
Evaluative couplet: Lance loves problem-solving, but not his own
Strophe 1: Is Lance's evaluation gendered?
   Stanza 1: PE frames his assumption as a question
   Stanza 2: Lance's qualified response

Q3
Part 1 (Lines 10–43) – A narrative of gendered learning in Lance's family:
'the women usually get what they want'
Strophe 1: Co-construction of the narrative theme
   Stanza 1: PE constructs Q3
   Stanza 2: Constructing the possibility of the opening narrative:
   Lance provides the focus, PE invites elaboration
Strophe 2: Narrative account of learning from family experience
   Stanza 3: Women's wants – an observation
   Stanza 4: Father's work – an explanation for waiting
   Stanza 5: An embedded but uncertain conclusion
Strophe 3: Emergence of a linked but new narrative theme
   Stanza 6: PE reconstructs Q3
   Stanza 7: Lance dismantles Q3, reflects, introduces own
   theme of stubbornness
Strophe 4: Narrative themes connect
   Stanza 8: PE reforms Q3 around Lance's new theme
   Stanza 9: Gendered wants/gendered jobs

Part 2 (Lines 44–80) – A narrative of gendered learning and identity
Strophe 5: Co-constructing a new narrative direction
   Stanza 10: PE recycles Q3 around contrast with Lance's sisters
   Stanza 11: School and work – gendered pathways
Strophe 6: Lance reflects on a 'canonical' rumour
   Stanza 12: Lance states and evaluates the rumour
   Stanza 13: 'Consequences': Lance links his re-evaluation of female
   cleverness and his own (male) behaviour –
   'offending … anything'
Strophe 7: The rabbit run – a narrative of gendered learning in Lance's family
   Stanza 14: Contrasting approaches –
   'a woman … my mum'/'My dad and me'
   Stanza 15: A personal narrative elaborating the contrast and embedding
   Lance's re-evaluation of the 'canonical' rumour
   Evaluative coda: 'women think more/they plan more'

Table 4.1 Continued

Strophe 8: Co-constructing further reflection on the gendered theme of cleverness

    Stanza 16: Lance wants to be 'clever' like 'a woman … my mum'

    Stanza 17: The choice of mentors

    Stanza 18: Evaluative coda – formulation of a developmental dilemma: ambivalence of cross-gender admiration

---

which he makes a clear evaluation (Stanza 12). In the context of this he introduces the theme of 'consequences', which (in terms of this non-offence-related interview) he gratuitously and critically links with his offending. Strophe 7 picks up and develops a narrative of learning gendered practices in Lance's family focused on the central theme of consequences or planning ahead, concluding with a revaluation of the 'canonical' rumour. In Strophe 8, Lance expresses a definite preference for his mother's kind of 'cleverness', then tempered by a dilemma of emotional investment in cross-gender admiration.

Thus, from PE's initial invitation to Lance to reflect on contrasts of gendered learning in his family, Lance's movement across this Part 2 stretch of text can be thought of as practising through narrative to situate himself and his wants as a boy in terms of gendered emotional attachments. He does this, we will argue, not just in general terms of 'love' for his mother, but in specific terms of his admiration for her kind of 'cleverness', a 'cleverness' he identifies generically *with* women and *as* an approach to behaviour that *avoids* the kind of inattention to consequences typical, he suggests, of his own male behaviour. Using Gee's (1991) focusing system and levels of narrative interpretation in the context of the interview as co-construction, we continue to demonstrate the means and potential of critical narrative analysis to develop closely warranted, extended and sustained thematic interpretation of discursive text, including, in this case, pursuing links between aspects of Lance's experience of gendered learning and the social construction of the problem of dangerous masculinity expressed by his sexually abusing other children.

Strophe 5: co-constructing a new narrative direction

Turning to the Part 2 text in Figure 4.1, it is evident that Stanzas 10 and 11, which compose Strophe 5, represent PE's recycling of Q3 and Lance's initial response to this. His opening 'So' and 'That's' mark transition in a number of ways. 'So WHAT OTHER THINGS' (l. 44) expresses a coherence with what has come before, but also a recognition that Lance's preceding 'Yeah', 'Um' and 'Yeah' (ll. 42–3) seem to indicate a winding down of that piece of conversation. On the other hand, the juxtaposition of 'OTHER THINGS' and 'That's ONE kind of thing/ you've LEARNED' indicates PE's intention still to pursue Q3 in the frame of a possible contrast about what might be 'DIFFERENT' between his own and his sisters' experience of 'GROWING UP in YOUR family' (l. 45).

The 3-second wait (l. 46) before Lance's response suggests a kind of thinking time that makes his opening 'Don't know' (l. 47), and the implied but absent psychological subject 'I', more like a point of verbal departure than an actual point of view; he is *not* unsure. In the fluency of his next five lines, Lance concisely outlines his view of two gendered pathways 'through the SCHOOL YEARS' – 'my SISTERS were/PUSHED HARDER...where ME and my BROTHER WEREN'T' (ll. 47–8). He then illustrates this in ll. 49–51, twice again using an 'it' construction for the psychological subject, suggesting something consistent or lasting enough to be experienced, albeit differently, as a 'given' state of affairs, the situation of his parents' predictable gendered positions 'through the SCHOOL YEARS'. Nevertheless, how Lance uses this construction in relation to 'ME and my BROTHER' differs from how he uses it in relation to 'my SISTERS'. The 'CASE' of the boys is constructed in terms of a 'they' (which includes himself) whose experience of their parents' attitude to their education is reported in a passive, third-party voice – 'if they WANT TO do the WORK/they'll DO IT,/IF they DON'T/they WON'T' (l. 49). The pitch glide emphases suggest an uncompromising contrast in WANT/DO, and DON'T/WON'T. One way of reading this could be that boys are intractable and cannot be influenced; another could be that boys are responsible for themselves but not accountable to others. The boys' third-party report suggests what they do or do not do is utterly conditional on whether they 'WANT TO' or not; with an immovable object, to be 'PUSHED HARDER' makes no sense, either to the object or to the would-be mover, son or parent.

This illustration contrasts strongly with the 'case' Lance reports of how his 'SISTERS were/PUSHED HARDER'. For them, 'it was a case of, YOU KNOW,/"You NEED TO DO THIS WORK/to get THROUGH and/to GET what you WANT"' (ll. 50–1). Lance reports this as an exhortation he has overheard so many times before it is ingrained in his memory like a broken record; he enters into a parental persona and his tone of voice becomes wheedling as he repeats what seems so obvious even PE may already know it ('it was a case of, YOU KNOW'). An undifferentiated parental voice addresses the gendered psychological subject, 'You', directly and prescriptively. The protracted pitch glide emphasis on 'NEED' in relation to 'TO DO THIS WORK', mimicking parental earnestness, contrasts in the overall flow of speech with Lance's pitch glide emphasis on 'WANT' (l. 49) in his case report of the boys. For the girls, the content of 'NEED' is spelled out at two levels and over two periods of time: at one level, the need to 'get THROUGH' emphasises both the importance of completing school and of doing at least well enough; at another level, 'to get THROUGH' is not an aim or end in itself, and this is made evident by repeating the word 'get' but with a new pitch glide emphasis in 'GET what you WANT'. To go 'THROUGH' school here is literally a passage into a future 'to GET what you WANT'. Implicit in this prescription is a subtext: *not* 'TO DO THIS WORK' and not to get 'THROUGH' deletes the 'and' connecting 'THROUGH' to 'GET' with the consequences that 'WANT' cannot be realised.

Lance's fluency seems suddenly to dry up rather than deliberately end after his parental imitation which is followed by a 5-second gap interrupted by a self-conscious 'um' that leads to no further comment (l. 51). Boys, Lance's account suggests, cannot be influenced because they are, or need to be, self-motivated, independent, autonomous 'motivators' in relation to their own wants. In the boys' case there appears to be no future-context, no implications or consequences to doing or not doing 'the WORK'. (In practice, the unfolding of Lance's narrative situating himself in relation to his mother and father will both belie and illustrate this myth of independence.) Girls, by contrast, depend on prescriptive nagging for their own good or else they are unlikely to persist or to succeed at getting what they want. In light of Part 1, for the girls to be 'PUSHED HARDER to go/through the SCHOOL YEARS' could be seen as basic training in the kind of strategic stubbornness Lance has suggested may explain his local experience 'That the WOMEN/usually GET/what they WANT'. It is not yet clear what the implications for men may be of a differently gendered pathway 'through the SCHOOL YEARS'.

Strophe 6: a 'canonical' rumour stated and evaluated

The duration of Lance's silence (l. 51) serves as a structural cue: PE begins to wonder about the meaning of what he has just been saying. PE's following question signifies an assumed coherence with ('So') and also a shift into the new Strophe 6 as he tries to nudge attention from the descriptive level of Lance's preceding narrative, alluded to globally as 'THAT', to a possible subtext of that narrative which interests him, 'WHAT does THAT mean/about being a BOY, then,/if you DO that?' (l. 52). Although Lance's initial unemphasised response, 'I don't know', locates himself as psychological subject, it does so less as a position than as a transition. Distancing him from school as the retrospective (Stanza 11) context of PE's question, the direction Lance's response does take (Stanza 12), after a 2-second pause (l. 53), represents a development of his own 'on-line' immediate and emerging thoughts. He introduces a major new theme, which at the same time picks up on a number of meanings implicit in his narrative of gendered learning so far, and which becomes central to the whole of Part 2.

Lance begins to strongly develop the direction of his thought but then interrupts himself with a speech disruption (l. 53). The shift of pitch glide emphasis from 'You know' in l. 53 to 'YOU KNOW' in l. 54 suggests that Lance's change of tack may have something to do with how he wants to involve if not co-opt PE, as listener, in what he is about to say. His first phrasing sounds like an assertion that, on its own, Lance may decide could risk being taken as his view. Cutting himself off at 'mo', Lance engages PE's attention with an incomplete suggestion. Then, recommencing with a new emphasis on 'YOU KNOW', he connects PE with what is coming, links him with both his own knowing and an inclusive, shared wider social context of 'this THING GOING ROUND', but commits neither himself nor PE to agreeing with the general rumour he reports (that 'there's this THING GOING ROUND that/MEN are supposed to be MORE CLEVER', l. 54), and repairs 'mo' with 'MORE CLEVER', presumably the same words he meant to say before but now in a reversed context with revised meaning. What was so significant for Lance that it called for this speech disruption? Along with how he may want to involve PE in hearing what he says, this reversal also reflects a shift of priorities that prepares for Lance's evaluation. If 'WOMEN AREN'T/SUPPOSED/ to BE', that is, if they are not 'allowed' or 'expected' to be, something particular, then, if they are, the case against them is *de facto*, and if they are not there is no case. But by reversing the context from what women are not supposed to be to what 'MEN are supposed to be', the shift of pitch glide emphasis away from 'SUPPOSED' to 'supposed' changes the meaning from one of a case against to a rumoured *assumption about*, an impersonal 'THING'. Lance situates himself in relation to a canonical assumption about the relative 'cleverness' of men and women, which he is assuming PE has heard. But in the flow of his expression, the purpose of stating this general rumour is to assert a counterhegemonic view that it 'is NOT ACTUALLY TRUE' (l. 55).

In his linguistic construction of these lines Lance displaces the psychological subject 'WOMEN' with 'THING', a construction similar to his earlier uses of 'it' suggesting something situational, 'given', a state of affairs, like gendered domestic arrangements around TV watching, dinner and parental attitudes towards school. In this impersonal context the counterview Lance asserts is also impersonal, a contradictory 'given' in relation to which, as himself a psychological subject, Lance declares no overtly personal perspective. Nevertheless, as with his other 'it' constructions, Lance's narrative can be thought of as a form of practising to critically situate (or practice in situating) himself and his wants in the context of this 'THING' 'which is NOT ACTUALLY TRUE'. The theme of gendered 'cleverness' has a bearing on Lance's thinking about gendered pathways through school, for example. If girls are not supposed to become clever women, then to 'get THROUGH and/to GET what you WANT' is no compliment but more like a survival tactic where consequences can be fatal and the meanings of 'NEED' are stark. If boys become clever men no matter what they do or do not do 'through the SCHOOL YEARS', then cleverness is like a gendered gene, an inherited mantle, a consequence of being male that simply supports the equivalence of wants and entitlements. Lance's experience and evaluation of his parents' cleverness, as well as his experience of school, is crucially important narrative material for discursively negotiating his own psychological perspective on 'this THING GOING ROUND'. In the remainder of Part 2, Lance situates himself primarily in relation to his parents' cleverness, and, as we will touch on, in Part 3 in relation to school.

But what exactly is it that Lance is saying 'is NOT ACTUALLY TRUE'? That men are more clever than women? That women are not more clever than men? PE is still left somewhat unsure about this after Lance's contrast with what is not true: 'Just as CLEVER/as what WOMEN are' (l. 56). Lance does not seem to be saying one is 'more clever' than the other, but rather that the rumour that 'MEN are supposed to be MORE CLEVER' is not true because 'ACTUALLY' men are not 'more' but simply 'just as' clever as women, equivalent not superior. It seems possible, however, that even here women rather than men are represented as the standard for that equivalence, men 'as CLEVER as' women rather than women as clever as men. While Lance demotes the assumption of men being cleverer, an assumption that is not apparently held by men only, he is elevating a view of women's cleverness that contradicts or at least challenges that assumption. PE's response at l. 57 seeks to reconnect Lance's comments with the original frame for Q3 about what 'you've LEARNED in your family' (l. 44) and at the same time to reflect back his understanding of what Lance has just been saying. Lance's 'Yeah', which seems to represent a validation of PE's understanding so far, and his ensuing 6-second pause which seems to indicate readiness to move the conversation on, have been transcribed across ll. 57–8 to signify a structural transition.

In Stanza 13 (ll. 58–60), Lance begins to distinguish in women's/ men's equivalent cleverness a significant difference in comparison specifically with himself. This difference, we argue, is of such importance for Lance that it becomes the central theme for the remainder of Part 2. Any acceptable interpretation of the text needs to address questions such as: Why is this difference important? Why is it important at this point in Lance's narrative? And, why does he make the apparently gratuitous connection of this difference, at this point, with 'the OFFENDING' and of all three with 'ANYTHING' (l. 60)?

Lance begins with a speech repair, 'a WOMA, a WOMAN'S', which suggests that his 'on-line' thinking and his verbalising are closely linked as he further develops his thoughts, that this is not a story in the process of repetition but of occasioned formation, and perhaps its articulation is part of his thinking. What for Lance distinguishes a woman's cleverness is that she is 'more likely to/THINK THINGS OUT' (l. 58). When Lance then contrasts this gendered cleverness with his 'ALWAYS/being TOLD ... /I HAVEN'T thought of the CONSEQUENCES of DOING something' (l. 59), he seems to accept the judgement of others that he lacks what in his view most characterises women's cleverness, but perhaps with some reflective awareness of his own family learning, that where 'WANT' not 'WORK' determines privilege consequences may seem to count for little. The implications of this in his own life, he is 'ALWAYS/being TOLD', are specific and far reaching, linked first to 'the OFFENDING' and then to 'ANYTHING'. Although 'I'm' in l. 59 stands as a grammatical subject, it is a representation of Lance as heard through what he is told by others about himself, not his own representation. Thus there is some dislocation and possible ambivalence between 'I'm' as a grammatical subject and a commitment to 'I'm' as a psychological subject. This continues in the tangential and anonymous way in which Lance links not thinking about 'the/CONSEQUENCES of DOING something' with 'NOT PARTICULARLY the OFFENDING, but,/you know, ANYTHING' (l. 60). All of this could be understood as minimising and resisting responsibility *vis à vis* offending. On the other hand, if Lance's narrative is thought about in terms of his practising to situate himself and his wants in relation to other relationships and other social perspectives, then this set of connections may indicate significant and 'on-line' reflection about a way of accounting for himself that fits with others' perceptions, fits with a kind of cleverness that might help to address the problem of consequences and recognises that this problem includes 'OFFENDING' within a broader continuum of 'ANYTHING' as part (so far at least) of a gendered way of living.

From feminist and social constructionist perspectives, this last possibility is particularly interesting: Lance seems to be reflecting on the possibility that the *absence* of a certain kind of, as he sees it, gendered cleverness or way of thinking from his life has consequences for whenever he is 'DOING something'. One reason that 'something' is 'NOT PARTICULARLY the OFFENDING' may be because, in this context, offending is simply *typical* of, rather than a deviance from, how as a boy he goes about 'DOING' 'ANYTHING'. The suggestion that these thoughts are in a process of formation, rather than a rehearsal, for instance, of 'defensive' or minimising stories, is supported by Lance's second false start, in l. 59 – 'TOLD, you know,/not, I HAVEN'T'. It is unclear whether this 'not' might be a prelude to another grammatical version of the phrase 'NOT PARTICULARLY the OFFENDING'. If so, and had it been inserted earlier in the sentence, this would have shifted the pitch glide emphases of new information so that 'the OFFENDING' was marginalised, alluded to in order to

leave it behind, rather than, as it is, taken up into the central connection between 'CONSEQUENCES of DOING' and 'ANYTHING'.

Strophe 7: building a rabbit run – a narrative of gendered learning

Lance's 2-second pause (l. 60) after these comments is more like coming up for air than a sign of a break in his flow of speech. PE, however, interjects just as Lance says 'Well', ready to continue;
recognising this PE apologises, and Lance immediately picks up from
his first 'Well' (l. 61) in a way that is coherent with what he has just
been saying and marks a structural shift into new focused material,
Strophe 7, Stanza 14. In l. 62, on rising pitch glides, Lance's second
'Well' sustains the centrality of 'a WOMAN' in his continuing narrative interest, and his third 'well' directs attention to a specific exemplary person, 'SAY MY MUM' (l. 62). Whereas narrative material in
Strophe 6 retained a high degree of generality, almost of theory,
Strophe 7 is anchored illustratively in highly specific family detail.
In Strophe 6, Lance can be thought of as situating himself in relation
to such broad themes as the equivalence and difference of gendered
cleverness, and gendered implications of forethought and consequences in relation to his own actions. In Strophe 7, through a
detailed story about his parents' gendered approaches to building a
rabbit run, Lance situates his differing emotional attachments to his
mother and father in a way that graphically illustrates the theme of
consequences and reinforces and amplifies his view that women
'THINK THINGS OUT'. It also sets the context for locating a major
developmental dilemma for Lance of cross-gender admiration.

In Strophe 7, Stanza 14, Lance introduces a broad comparison
between how his 'MUM' is 'more LIKELY/to PLAN something OUT',
and how 'MY DAD and ME/it's, you know, HANDS ON,/want to GET
IN there/DOING SOMETHING' (ll. 63–4). These lines serve as a kind
of abstract for Stanza 15 where this comparison is elaborated in detail
through an example – 'like, for INSTANCE,/MAKING a RUN/which
was JUST for our RABBIT' (l. 65). Between l. 62 and l. 68 Lance's fluency continues unabated with only occasional 'Uhum's' and 'Yeah's'
from PE. After the two false starts in ll. 58 and 59, the direction and
clarity of his expression is sure and confident until the Evaluative
Coda at l. 68 when, after some thought, he returns to a categorical

judgement about 'WOMEN' rounding off and bringing to an end this narrative illustration.

The pitch glide emphases in ll. 62–3 (Stanza 14) – WOMAN/SAY MY MUM/SHE'S LIKELY/PLAN OUT – plainly carry forward in the person of his mother the key theme from Stanza 13 that 'a WOMAN'S more likely to/THINK THINGS OUT' (l. 58). That is, these emphases function structurally to maintain the cohesion of his developing narrative. The contrasting pitch glide emphases in l. 64 – MY DAD ME/HANDS ON/GET IN/DOING SOMETHING – add and embed new information which, at the same time, carries forward the theme of 'the CONSEQUENCES of DOING something'. Although this information suggests something about Lance's relationship with his father, its purpose here – that is, addressing the question, Why is this important? – is to elaborate on his central theme about 'a WOMAN ... MY MUM'. The new information could be thought of as a foil to his main concern to situate himself in relation to a gendered cleverness characterised by planning things out. Lance firmly locates or identifies himself in relation to each parent by the emphasised 'MY MUM' and 'MY DAD and ME', suggesting he is on familiar ground about which he is an authority. Through his identification with his father he shares both in a difference from his mother, who is 'more LIKELY/to PLAN something OUT', and in a similarity to his father, 'HANDS ON,/want to GET IN there/DOING SOMETHING'.

The contrast set up in Stanza 14 between Lance's mother's and father's approaches to doing something is echoed and elaborated in Stanza 15, structurally signalled by a shift from the general to a particular 'for INSTANCE' (l. 65). Stanza 14 represents the context in which this 'INSTANCE' is to be understood, including in that context the thematic material being carried forward from Stanza 13. In Stanza 15, an onomatopoeic parallel can clearly be heard between the descriptions of two gendered approaches to 'MAKING a RUN' and the language Lance uses to express those descriptions (see ll. 65–8).

The language Lance uses to describe how his dad and he go about 'DOING SOMETHING' is staccato and action-packed as the pitch glide emphases show: PLAN TO GO DOWN/GO DOWN SHOPS/BUY WOOD/CAGE/BRING/MAKE IT (l. 66). The verbs are transitive – plan, go, buy, bring, make – and the action is task-focused – shops, wood, cage. There are implicit instrumental assumptions that 'we' know what to do, what to get and how to do it reflecting, perhaps, such wider discourses of power as 'we have the technology', problem solving and masculine rational action. No complications are foreseen, that is, apparently no 'CONSEQUENCES' need to be considered. The task done is its own criterion; the knowers and the doers are men bonded by the work. In this context the word 'PLAN' does not mean what his mother does 'to PLAN something OUT' (l. 63). When 'ME and my DAD' 'PLAN' there seems to be such a foreshortening of thinking and action that 'PLAN' does not include the need or time for the gendered observation that women 'THINK THINGS OUT' (l. 58).

The language Lance uses to describe his mother's approach to 'MAKING a RUN' is, by contrast, legato; on the whole, the pitch glide emphases and the words themselves are longer (l. 67). The verbs – DRAWING/COUNTING – are durative: there is a sense of time that precedes literally 'MAKING a RUN' when the 'MAKING' is being cal-culated in terms of design as well as of 'CONSEQUENCES' such as 'NEED' and 'COST'. Although, in the broader context of the preced-ing stanzas this narrative can be read as a positive illustration of a kind of gendered cleverness (one that Lance admires in his mother and the absence of which in his own life he has already linked to his problem of not thinking about 'the CONSEQUENCES of DOING something'), nevertheless Lance seems to register some ambivalence, some frustration with his mother's approach, which comes through in the slightly pedantic feel of 'PEN OUT'/'LITTLE SKETCHES', and 'COUNTING OUT THE LENGTHS of WOOD'. It is as if the language available to Lance for describing what his father and he do fits more comfortably with a 'masculine' approach which is energetic, excited, about which he expresses some enthusiasm yet which he does not admire; while the language he uses to describe what his mother does retains a slightly trivialising tone out of tune with his sense of admiration for her.

Discursively situating himself through narrative in relation to his mother/women is a complex activity. It involves uses of language that both express and construct differences of Lance's emotional attachments to his parents as individuals and investment in his own understanding of his experiences of what their gendered approaches to 'DOING SOMETHING' mean for him as a boy growing up in his family. These relationships represent and contribute to Lance's gendered sense-making of his own experience, both in relation to

'DOING' 'ANYTHING' and, included in this, in relation to 'the OFFENDING'. Lance does not reduce the complexity of his own narrative to an 'INSTANCE' of simple polarities; it is not *about* others, but an *activity* of his own. He is, in effect, 'DOING SOMETHING' in the process of his conversation which is *different* from what he is 'ALWAYS/being TOLD', he is practising how to think and how to speak, in the context of primary emotional attachments, about 'the/CONSEQUENCES of DOING'.

In the face of his own thinking, what we have called Lance's Evaluative Coda (l. 68) is structurally distinguished from Stanza 15 by the first significant hesitations in his flow of speech since l. 58. The contrast between his mother's and father's approaches to 'MAK-ING a RUN' have illustrated the general point that his mother is 'more LIKELY/to PLAN something OUT', he and his father 'to GET IN there/DOING SOMETHING'. But the illustration includes no evalua-tion of itself except, linguistically, to perhaps suggest some ambiva-lence towards or trivialising of his mother's approach. Lance's initial 2-second hesitation may represent some 'on-line' decision-making about whether or not he will situate himself in relation to his own narrative in terms of a 'Don't know' location. During his two follow-ing 2-second hesitations, he seems to decide instead to situate him-self and what he knows in terms of his narrative by stating the evaluative conclusion: 'so WOMEN THINK MORE...They PLAN MORE'. Although his use of 'so' ensures that the pitch glide empha-sis on 'WOMEN THINK MORE' is heard as following from what has come before, situating himself in relation to *this* conclusion was apparently not inevitable but decided. The evaluation does not sim-ply repeat his earlier views that women think things out (l. 58) or are more likely to plan something out (l. 63), though it picks these up. It specifically links thinking and planning with gendered practices, thus clearly defining in what way Lance thinks women are 'clever'; and it implicitly reinforces a difference between this kind of clever-ness and the message Lance gets that 'I HAVEN'T thought of the/CONSEQUENCES of DOING something'.

Strophe 8: co-constructing further reflection on the gendered theme of cleverness

Wanting to be clearer about what the evaluative significance of Lance's conclusion may mean for him, at l. 69 PE asks his first question since l. 57. This is linked by his global 'THAT'S' to what Lance has just been saying, and signifies a structural shift to Strophe 8 by introducing a related yet new theme in Stanza 16 – the effect of Lance's experience and evaluation on his 'VIEW/of the kind of BOY, YOUNG MAN,/YOU want to BECOME?' This question could be heard as a reflective one in terms of the pitch glide emphasis on BOY, or as a future-oriented one in terms of the equal emphasis on YOUNG MAN. Lance picks it up immediately (across ll. 70–2) as reflective and develops a narrative in the past tense that also illustrates a continuing gendered view of himself and of his wants.

Lance seems to gain a moment of thinking time in the 'um' (l. 70) after his unemphasised 'Don't know', before positioning himself in terms of strongly emphasised new material. Here both the content of his assertion, of what he wanted ('TO BE able to PLAN') and how long he has wanted it ('ALWAYS'), that is, the suggestion that he has never not wanted it, are accomplished simultaneously by pitch glide emphases that serve in effect to clarify what PE's opening question ('affected YOUR VIEW') means for him. Lance replaces PE's 'BECOME' (l. 69) and its developmental implications, with his 'I ALWAYS/WANTED TO BE'. In this construction Lance is the psychological subject of a desired ability ('TO BE able to PLAN') experienced in the enduring duration of 'ALWAYS' characterised not by 'BECOME' but by 'BE'. Furthermore, what he 'ALWAYS/WANTED TO BE' contrasts with what he is 'ALWAYS being TOLD' (l. 59). Thus, PE's developmental framework of 'BECOME' is reconstructed in terms of a desired ability that situates Lance and his wants in relation to his mother in such a way that what he has *not* become is what she represents and what he has become is *not* what he wants to 'BE'. There seems to be no language by which to construct how to *become* what he wants to *be*, no sense of becoming that could involve different consequences informing different identities.

The speech repair in l. 71 ('det' repaired to 'DETAIL') is also a false start in that it seems to redirect or interrupt the grammatical logic of Lance's 'on-line' thinking. Why does not the line, for example, just run: 'plan things out in good detail'? Between ll. 70 and 72 there seems to be a kind of dysphasia operating between Lance's thinking, in which he is making a shift from the general ('I ALWAYS/WANTED TO BE able to PLAN') to the particular ('like GOOD DETAIL'), and the language available to him to express that thinking or view in 'speakings'. His initial response to PE's question enacts a shift into a narrative frame of explanation. The time frame set up for this explanation is situationally defined in terms of 'WHATEVER HAPPENS' so time as duration, past, present and future, is implicit in the retrospective example that follows (Stanza 17). After perhaps somewhat trivialising how his mother planned the rabbit run with 'LITTLE SKETCHES', Lance may now be recalibrating his ambivalent admiration for her both in the evaluative idea of 'GOOD DETAIL' and the sense of her reliability/dependability, which is also present in 'WHATEVER HAPPENS'.

Structurally, Stanza 17 is signified in terms of the narrative commencement of an example which Lance introduces as 'if I was, like, TAKE,/ONCE...' (l. 73). Although this example is carried forward from the point of view of 'I' (ll. 73, 74, 75) as the psychological subject, and the two uses of 'if' (ll. 73/74) indicate exemplary rather than hypothetical situations, there remains an ambiguity at the centre of Lance's story: 'for SOME reason'. While 'some' suggests there *is* reason it at the same time *begs what* reason. Does Lance have a reason? Does he want or not want to say it? Or even to know it? In the context of these questions, the muted and momentary psychological subject 'you' (l. 73) may suggest some initial ambivalence about whether Lance will move in generic or domestic, impersonal or personal directions here. But, with the return to 'I' (l. 74), in the tacit context of school and homework, Lance is clearly stating at one level in this stanza that when he is 'PLANNING OUT/MAKING SOMETHING' to 'HAND...IN' he will 'ALWAYS CHECK IT with my MUM FIRST, you know' (l. 75), presumably before handing it in. This practice specifically excludes his father – 'NOT my DAD' – for reasons not elaborated on but implied by the gendered link between how his father goes about 'DOING SOMETHING' and the kind of help for 'PLANNING OUT/MAKING SOMETHING' that, for instance, his schoolwork required. In contrast, Lance twice states that he will 'LET HER (LET my MUM) READ THROUGH IT' (ll. 75/76), which almost suggests he is doing her a favour rather than asking her for help. Indeed, while on the one hand he seems to express a more direct appreciation of the kind of 'GOOD DETAIL' which in his own 'PLANNING OUT' his mother can 'CHECK' and help him to improve, on the other hand, he seems ambivalent/unsure or unwilling to be specific about this as his reason, rather than just 'SOME reason', for asking for her help. Lance recognises that his mother has abilities that help him, but at the same time he does not offer this as his reason for asking her for help. Her help and his need for her help seem to be conceptually and emotionally divorced, although they are in practice virtually synonymous, and this obscures his dependence on her dependability.

Lance is not unaware of the explanatory dilemma he has put himself in as he practices situating himself and this behaviour in relation to his mother in Stanza 18 (ll. 77–9). As if unhappy with the unspecific 'SOME reason', Lance proposes two elaborate possible reasons for why 'I'D ALWAYS CHECK IT with my MUM FIRST'. Structurally, these lines signify a new stanza because they are thematically coherent reflections on, in effect, Why does he do this?, and because they raise the focal question, Why in terms of the unfolding of his narrative is this so important? Lance locates himself, 'I', as a psychological subject across the stanza (ll. 77/79/80), but in each case in relation to a disclaimer – twice, 'I don't know', and once 'I WOULDN'T say'. His not knowing permits speculation about 'WHETHER it's BECAUSE' one thing or 'WHETHER it's because' another (ll. 77/78); they can be voiced both to himself and to the listener while committing him to neither, and, like any stories, they can draw attention to certain possibilities while omitting or occluding attention to others. Neither, for example, clearly recognises his own self-interest or dependence, to 'HAND...IN' a better piece of work with the help of his mother.

The first 'reason' – that Lance may ask his mother 'BECAUSE/SHE would have THOUGHT MORE ABOUT IT' – is consistent with his earlier gendered evaluative conclusion that 'WOMEN THINK MORE...They PLAN MORE' (l. 68). That is what women are like, so that is what he expects from his mother, why he asks and what he gets. This explanation is both personal and impersonal at once, and it is illogical. Although 'SHE' is clearly his mother, the assumption that 'SHE would have THOUGHT MORE ABOUT IT' also typifies a broader impersonal assumption about women that Lance seems to be in part generalising from his experience of using his mother's help. The explanation is illogical in that his mother cannot have 'THOUGHT MORE ABOUT IT' than Lance before he asks her to 'CHECK IT' or 'READ THROUGH IT', even if she may do so after he asks/lets her. Lance appears to credit his mother with a kind of impersonal, gendered 'THOUGHT' that is on tap for the asking because she is a woman. For him to depend on this does not seem to suggest his dependence on her, but perhaps a different 'instrumental' or strategic cleverness of his own to see and to make good use of what she *qua* woman does, 'THINK MORE...PLAN MORE'.

This possibility seems to be implicit in Lance's second and even more complex 'reason' for asking his mother's help. Here he suggests that in the act of asking her for help he is actually engaged in testing her, and through her testing the canonical 'rumour' about 'the LESS CLEVER TYPE' (l. 53 repeated at l. 78). In this way, Lance's invitation to his mother to 'CHECK IT' constitutes not help but a test 'to SEE IF SHE could FOLLOW the INSTRUCTIONS' (l. 79), to see if 'SHE' can follow what Lance has already done *by himself* but will now 'LET'/ allow her to read through. Is this test to show she is less clever, cleverer, just as clever or differently clever? Having struggled to express a gendered view of cleverness in which men are not more but 'just as CLEVER/as what WOMEN are' (l. 56), here Lance situates his own cleverness hierarchically in relation to his mother, testing whether she can follow the instructions for the work he asks her to 'CHECK'. Nevertheless, the standard for or category of this cleverness remains female, characterised more by thought and planning than simply by 'HANDS ON, want to GET IN there/DOING SOMETHING' (l. 64).

With these two reasons Lance situates himself and his wants in relation to a kind of gendered cleverness that simultaneously signifies what 'I ALWAYS/WANTED TO BE' (l. 70) and yet that does not mix him up with 'this THING GOING ROUND' about 'the LESS CLEVER TYPE'. But the position is precarious. On the one hand, he is in effect testing for cleverness 'so to SEE IF' it is there in his mother; on the other, he is expecting the same cleverness as a dependable resource to 'CHECK' his own work for 'GOOD DETAIL' so it will be more like what he 'ALWAYS WANTED'. There is an uneasy alliance between Lance's admiring view of his mother's cleverness and his view of himself as 'Just as CLEVER'. To the extent that her (woman's) cleverness is what he 'ALWAYS WANTED', it is in practice a cleverness he identifies with more by its absence in his life than its presence – 'I'm ALWAYS/being TOLD...I HAVEN'T thought of the/CONSEQUENCES of DOING something' (l. 59). To the extent that Lance situates himself and his wants in relation to this cleverness, what he wants to be and also what he is not are both represented by his mother's/women's cleverness. While both explanations (for why Lance asks his mother to check his work) turn on his admiration for the kind of cleverness she represents, they obscure his dependence on his mother and instead suggest an instrumental use of her and/or a hierarchical testing of her. Admiration and devaluation mix so that Lance himself feels the need to reclaim in PE's eyes the value of what he admires, correcting any possibility of misapprehension with the disclaimer 'I WOULDN'T say mum's STUPID' (l. 80). This disclaimed negative supports his positive assertions about women's cleverness – 'WOMEN THINK MORE … PLAN MORE' – in the person of his mother, but does so leaving the ambivalent impression that maybe his evaluation confers this cleverness or maybe his evaluation represents what he lacks but 'ALWAYS WANTED'.

Throughout Strophe 8 (Stanzas 16, 17, 18), Lance is developing his response to PE's question about how he thinks his evaluation (l. 68) that women think and plan more, has affected his 'VIEW/of the kind of BOY, YOUNG MAN,/YOU want to BECOME' (l. 69). The effects he narrates, focused on his struggles with admiration and devaluation, express a developmental dilemma, an ambivalent experience of himself and his wants (as a 'BOY, YOUNG MAN') in the context of cross-gender admiration for his mother's/women's cleverness. This admiration seems to teeter on the edge either of devaluing his father or of devaluing himself, of his mother seeming too powerful in relation to his father, or of his mother seeming clever in ways that highlight not so much what Lance wants but what Lance is not. In turn, this precarious situation may be addressed to accomplish an empowered view of himself either by marginalising his father's presence and kind of cleverness, or by devaluing his mother to such an extent through ignoring his dependence on her cleverness that Lance finds himself needing to explain that this exemplary woman, 'MY MUM', is actually not 'STUPID'. We suggest that Lance is struggling not so much with difficulties of narration or articulateness, as with the constraints of language and available discourses by which to make sense of his experience and emotional development so that he can construct a coherent, multifaceted story (anchored in domestic particulars with potential for social generality) of admiration for a woman's ways of thinking that includes a sense both of himself as a 'BOY, YOUNG MAN' and of a gendered cleverness that he has 'ALWAYS WANTED'.

Part 2: narrative practices of available, contestable and alternative gendered subject positions

Our thematic interpretation suggests Part 2 of Q3 coheres around the central theme of gendered cleverness. This theme is not simply polarised around male and female, represented by father and mother. To the extent that language is itself social practice, in the elaboration of his narrative material, Lance is involved in actively situating himself in relation both to an identity he clearly shares with his father ('MY DAD and ME') and an aspiration/desire for a kind of cleverness focused in terms of 'a WOMAN, you know,/well, SAY MY MUM'. The identity he shares with his father is further connected to gendered ways of 'DOING SOMETHING' which do not think 'of the/CONSE-QUENCES of DOING something', ways on a gendered continuum that include 'NOT PARTICULARLY the OFFENDING, but,/you know, ANYTHING' – ways, that is, which can be construed explicitly and implicitly as male, normative, problematic and dangerous to self and to others. The admiration he expresses for his mother's/women's cleverness is connected to a gendered thinking and planning which precedes the 'HANDS ON' with attention, in effect, to 'CONSEQUENCES' – action emerges from and is connected to a wider context of issues, responsibilities and relationships; achievement is not its only or even principal rationale.

We have suggested that there is an ambivalence for Lance about how to construct an inclusive, coherent view of himself in his gendered identity with his father and of himself in his cross-gender admiration for his mother's/women's cleverness. What his mother has, perhaps, worked out in terms of getting what she wants by means of more and less stubbornness, Lance has not worked out effectively for himself. Getting what he wants in terms of sexually abusing other children demonstrates in a glaring and unacceptable way not getting what he wants in relation to doing 'ANYTHING', that is, not getting a kind of cleverness that he says he 'ALWAYS WANTED', a cleverness his text suggests could be construed as safer both to self and to others. Lance's difficulty in situating himself in relation to this kind of cleverness can be thought of in terms of constitutive discourses of developmental norms. The theme of cross-gender admiration can be read as Lance personally having problems with socially sanctioned discourses of masculine sexual identity and experiencing complications with prescriptions for adolescent individuation and separation. On the other hand, it can be read in the context of dominant discourses of gendered identities which Lance is experiencing as problematic for himself and not fitting with what he most admires and wants to be more like himself. He may both experience himself as 'failing' in relation to these identities and at the same time be interrogating them for alternatives acceptable to himself and to others.

Connell (1987: 220), historicising personal identity in terms of 'life history', argues that 'complexities of personal life arise from structural contradictions that go far beyond the particular person'. The focusing systems of Lance's text so far have suggested a variety of complexities involved in his struggle through narrative to situate himself as a boy (both child and male) in relation to a kind of cleverness he sees in his mother and that he generalises to women. In particular, the ambivalence of his admiration for and devaluation of his mother makes sense in this wider context of gendered developmental norms. These norms can be seen to encourage the very approach to 'DOING SOMETHING' that discourages accountability for 'CONSEQUENCES' and personal responsibility. For instance, how Lance and his father go about building the rabbit run illustrates a project in which action, to 'just MAKE IT', 'to GET IN there/DOING SOMETHING', is the horizon of masculine responsibility. But by gratuitously connecting this kind of action with 'ALWAYS/being TOLD ... / ... I HAVEN'T thought of the/CONSEQUENCES of DOING something ... NOT PARTICULARLY the OFFENDING, but,/ ... ANYTHING', Lance locates a complexity in his own experience which reflects a broader structural contradiction. If 'OFFENDING', in his own observation, is on a continuum with 'ANYTHING' then, as Connell (1987: 107) puts it, '(far) from being a deviation from the social order, it is in a significant sense an enforcement of it'.

In this light, for Lance to express admiration for his mother's/ women's cleverness increases the complexities of his situation: there appear to be no normative or acceptable discourses available through which to practice views of himself and his wants that include both his identification with his father as masculine and identification with a kind of cleverness socially devalued for him as a boy by virtue of being connected to his mother/women. From a normative perspective Lance could be described perhaps as having separation/ individuation and/or gender identity problems. From the perspective of his own text, however, Lance's ambivalence itself stems from deliberately situating both Parts 1 and 2 of Q3 primarily in relation to women, in particular his mother and to some extent his sisters. His reasons for doing this constitute the overall thematic develop-ment of the text viewed as the co-construction of narrative material. Lance's mother seems to represent for him what he most admires and would like to be like, as well as what, by its absence in his life, most characterises him both as male and, as a male sexual abuser, dangerous.

In this regard, however, Connell's (1987: 183) observation is inter-esting:

> Hegemonic masculinity is always constructed in relation to various subordinated masculinities as well as in relation to women.

The same 'form of masculinity' that, for instance, devalues and then locates in women expressions of 'affective action' (Seidler, 1994: 28) in contrast to 'rational action' identified with independence and masculinity, also devalues these in boys. Consequently, processes of subordination of women are repeated not only through various adult 'subordinated masculinities' but also through the institutionalisation (e.g. school, a theme Lance picks up again in Part 3) of developmen-tal discourses constitutive of gendered childhood and reproductions of patriarchy. From this perspective, Lance's choice to situate himself and his wants in relation to his mother and to his generalisations about women cannot simply be explained away as a phase in the separa-tion paradigm without ignoring the coherence of his textual cues and focusing systems. Taking these into account, the coherence of his responses around his ambivalent admiration/devaluation of his mother's/women's cleverness effectively constitutes him, in relation to hegemonic masculinity, as a boy member of some subordinated masculinity. Whether this 'membership' constitutes an interrogation of or resistance to hegemonic masculinity is another question. But, by situating himself and his wants in relation to women, in this text Lance is practising through narrative a form of masculinity that dif-fers enough from the norm, for example, for him to have noticed that 'there's this THING GOING ROUND that/MEN are supposed to be MORE CLEVER' and to take issue with it as 'NOT ACTUALLY

TRUE'. Perhaps his ambivalence is as understandable as taking issue with this 'THING' is exceptional.

At the same time, however, it has to be said that this line of reasoning could locate Lance in another form of subordinated masculinity, the sexual offender, individualised, pathologised, criminalised and marginalised as 'them' in contrast to a hegemonic 'us'. What is the difference, if there is a difference? If sexually abusing, amongst other forms of interpersonal violence, can be seen to articulate and reinforce hegemonic masculinity, as feminists and others suggest, then what might Lance's admiration for his mother's kind of cleverness that thinks and plans in relation to 'CONSEQUENCES' mean for him? We suggest that, in part, Lance locates his admiration for his mother's cleverness in contrast to, and possibly as a solution for, the dangerous 'HANDS ON' action of masculinity that he associates both with his own 'OFFENDING' as well as 'ANYTHING' he does. Does he situate himself in order to practice a different possibility for a subordinated but safe and non-offending masculinity? At the same time, however, he may also be cunningly locating himself in relation to that same kind of cleverness in order to groom other children for abuse and to construct systems of secrecy and self-protection that represent highly sophisticated attention to 'CONSEQUENCES'.[1]

Rather than interpret this as a contradiction, it may be more fruitful to consider the possibility that his ambivalence may provide a context for meaning-making within which not offending *can* make

1. There are important thematic connections that deserve further consideration between Lance's expressed admiration for his mother as thinker/ planner, qualities which in this context he suggests that he lacks, and the energetic, instrumental and clear way in which he talks about 'grooming' during his offence-related interview. He himself sees this process as involving very careful planning, very detailed thinking about consequences so that secrecy is well in place and also a system of 'back ups' to cover his tracks in case an abusive initiative raises some alarm. In the context of his sexually abusive behaviours, Lance is an accomplished thinker and planner with a sharp eye to consequences. From a clinical perspective, then, the unstable practices of subject positioning evident, for instance, across our Part 2 stretch of text, suggest strong research support for therapeutic approaches exploring implications, responsibilities and effects of choices amongst available and alternative personal and social narratives constitutive of gendered practices ranging from 'offending' to non-offending (e.g. Jenkins, 1990; Elms, 1990).

important and gendered sense, instead, for instance, of 'reading' ambivalence as lack of commitment to change and/or a sign of pathology. Connell (1995: 76) argues:

> 'Hegemonic masculinity' is not a fixed character type, always and everywhere the same. It is, rather, the masculinity that occupies the hegemonic position in a given pattern of gender relations, a position always contestable.

To the extent that Lance is engaged in situating himself in relation to a kind of cleverness he identifies with women and that differs from his 'OFFENDING' as well as 'ANYTHING' he does, he may at times be contesting while at other times occupying a position of hegemonic masculinity, a position which in large part sustains itself through social narratives that obscure alternative choices of masculine identities and mask the fissures or structural contradictions of that hegemony. What can be seen to contest, what can be seen to contribute to, the pattern of gender relations that Lance differentiates from his mother's cleverness, 'the masculinity that occupies the hegemonic position'? To some extent Lance's central themes construct a developing response to Q3 in which canonical ingredients contributing to his personal narratives seem to limit and muddle Lance's experience and discursive negotiations of masculine identity. These ingredients promote approaches to learning that link masculinity to expressions of power through action-without-consequences and through entitlements. Furthermore, where responsibility for consequences is disqualified as being gender-biased to women, does this feminise accountability and guilt and thus fail to offer Lance as a boy available subject positions of accountable masculinity which are at the same time capable of mutuality in contrast to 'power-based behaviours or thoughts' (Ryan and Lane, 1997: 84)? To what extent in the fabric and ambivalence of Lance's narrative may there be any basis, for example, through some therapeutic approaches, for the co-construction of replacement discourses?

Using the Part 2 stretch of Q3 text, we have demonstrated the kind of close and extended textual work necessary to doing thematic interpretation anchored in the 'trace in the talk'. As we have said, our aim is to be illustrative not comprehensive, nor are we claiming an 'essentialist' single interpretation of the interview as co-construction or of the particular ways we have privileged Lance's sense-making. With this in mind, we will conclude our analysis of Q3 stepping back from highly detailed analysis and focusing instead across Part 3 (ll. 81–145) in broad terms of connected chunks or portions of the interview, with a view to further foregrounding cultural themes 'speaking' through the text.

5
Canonical Narratives and Cultural Orders: Moving Analysis to a More Molar Level

Aims: accounting for thematic coherence across 'headline' patterns – a narrative of gendered schooling for the world of work

In this chapter, we explore the way in which narratives can be examined in terms of the relationships between more 'molar' parts of the material, with a view particularly to identifying the effects of cultural discourses. For example, we suggest that in the course of the interview we have analysed, Lance carries the Part 2 theme of gendered 'cleverness' forward into Part 3 through school as a significant institutional context where linguistic and social practices, organised around developmental discourses constitutive of gendered childhood and reproductions of patriarchy, are thematically linked with contesting hegemonic and subordinated constructions of masculine identities. This broader approach is facilitated by use of macro-linguistic transcription tools (Stanzas, Strophes and Parts) signifying discursive coherence, which provide a 'trail' or account of interpretive headlines.

We organise our following discussion around a broad three-part structural movement across the Part 3 text (ll. 81–144) reproduced in Figure 5.1.

Figure 5.1 A narrative of gendered schooling

Part 3
(A narrative of gendered schooling for the world of work)
Strophe 9

Figure 5.1   Continued

(Co-constructing the narrative frame)
Stanza 19
(PE recycles Q3 around the imperative 'ought')
81. *PE*: Yeah, yeah. (3 secs)/SO, in AGAIN,/just THINKING about GROWING UP in your FAMILY,
82. what OTHER kinds of THINGS/would you say you've LEARNED/about BEING a BOY,
83. what BOYS SHOULD BE,/what they OUGHT TO BECOME?
84. *L*: I don't know, like, you know, what BOYS should BECOME and that,

Stanza 20
(L's shifts narrative frame from 'ought to become' to 'want' and 'try')
85. you know, MUM and DAD, you know,/they HAVEN'T really PUSHED US INTO/what we SHOULD become.
86. It's a CASE of, you know,/'What do you WANT to BECOME?'.
    PE: Right
87. *L*: You know, whatever you WANT to become/you GO ROUND and TRY/to BECOME THAT./
88. *PE*: Right. So they've supported you in TRYING
    L: Yeah/
    PE: what you WANTED to DO?
    L: Yeah.

Strophe 10
(Evaluating the narrative frame)
Stanza 21
(L contrasts 'should' with 'nice')
89. Um, you know, they HAVEN'T SAID
90. 'OH, YOU SHOULD go/into THIS line of WORK', you know,
91. which has been NICE.
    PE: WHAT'S been NICE about THAT?
92. *L*: Um, YEAH, as I SAY,/PESTERING, you know,

Stanza 22
(Illustrating 'nice': the covert 'ought' of independence and choice)
93. like DURING the OPTIONS,/you know, when you have to CHOOSE your THREE SUBJECTS
    PE: Yeah, yeah
94. *L*: INSTEAD of being TOLD, you know/'YOU SHOULD do/THIS one and THIS one and THIS one
95. so you can GO and DO, BE a WHATEVER'
    PE: Yeah
96. *L*: it's a CASE OF, you know,/'THINK about it for yourSELF and/MAKE your OWN DECISIONS'.
(Coda)
 97. THAT'S what I mean by NICE. ??
    PE: THAT'S the kind of THING/you mean by NICE?
    L: Uhum

Figure 5.1   Continued

Strophe 11
(Elaborating the theme of 'nice' in terms of choice)
Stanza 23
(Following the theme of choice: from abstraction to example)
  98. *PE*: And did, did you FEEL/that you were GIVEN
  99. AS MUCH FREEDOM TO CHOOSE as you wanted or/TOO MUCH FREE-
       DOM TO CHOOSE as you wanted?
  100. *L*: No, ENOUGH freedom.
       PE: Enough?
       L: Yeah,/but NOT TOO MUCH.
       PE: Yeah.
       L: You know, JUST ENOUGH. (2 secs)
  101. Like, I don't KNOW,/HOW would you put it/into EXAMPLES NOW?
       PE: Uhum
  102. *L*: Like DOING the OPTIONS again
       PE: Yeah

Stanza 24
(L's narrative of supported choice: 'ask' not 'should' helps to distinguish 'wrong' from right choices)
  103. *L*: you know, if I was THINKING/about doing SOMETHING, um,/WRONG,
  104. you know, they'll GO and/so they ASK ME,/
  105. 'WHY do I want to do THAT for?'
       PE: Yeah
  106. *L*: 'Now, WHEN is that,/WHY is that going to HELP me get a JOB I WANTED
       TO?' You know
Coda
(L's 'options' choices guided through parental questioning)
  107. *PE*: So, THEY were asking/THOSE SORTS of QUESTIONS?
  108. *L*: Yeah, to make SURE I CHOSE/in the RIGHT OPTIONS./
       PE: RIGHT. (2 secs)

Strophe 12
(Negotiating the theme of gender difference in relation to choice)
Stanza 25
(PE's raises the theme of gender difference through questioning the 'similar' in L's family: L relocates this theme in terms of 'school is different')
  109. *PE*. And do you THINK,/were your SISTERS treated/in a SIMILAR kind of
       WAY/would you SAY?
       L: Yeah.
  110. *PE*: That FREEDOM/and then that SUPPORT/to think it THROUGH/for
       themSELVES?
       L: Yeah
  111. *PE*: So THAT was SIMILAR/for THEM as GIRLS/and for YOU as a
       BOY/GROWING UP in your FAMILY?
       L: Yeah.
       PE: Uhu, yeah./

Figure 5.1   Continued

112. *L*: MIND you,/SCHOOL is DIFFERENT/ISN'T IT,/for BOYS and GIRLS?

Stanza 26
(PE follows L who elaborates on gendered 'subjects')
113. *PE*: Yeah, WHAT are some of the DIFFERENCES/you've LEARNED?
114 As you've been GROWING UP in your FAMILY/and GOING to these SCHOOLS,/what have you LEARNED about those DIFFERENCES/
115. that you just said between GIRLS and BOYS?
116. *L* : You know, IT'S/sort of THINGS,/the SUBJECTS,/you know, where GIRLS will stick to NETBALL/when the BOYS will do RUGBY.
      PE: Uhu/
117. *L*: You know, and DURING TECHNOLOGY/the GIRLS/will DO TEXTILES and FOOD/where the BOYS/will do CDT and CRAFTS.
      PE: Yeah
      L: Yeah.

Strophe 13
(A different difference: L's negotiation of gendered 'subjects')
Stanza 27
(What and how L chose)
118. *PE*: And is, is THAT what YOU DID?
119. Did you FOLLOW that kind of SAME PATTERN?
120. *L*: NO, I DIDN'T actually,
121. I went and done FOOD for TECHNOLOGY.
      PE: DID you?
122. HOW did you MANAGE to do/something SO DIFFERENT from/what the OTHER ones were DOING?/
123. *L*: You know, they GIVE me an OPTIONS SHEET
      PE: Yeah/
124. *L*: ?? you get and CHOOSE/what you WANTED.
      PE: Yeah.

Stanza 28
(L's narrative reflection on making his 'different' choice)
125. *L*: You know, but DURING the,/FILLING IN the/OPTIONS SHEET/I was STILL THINKING,/you know,
126. 'I'M going to,/if I GO FOR THAT,/I'm going to be the ONLY BOY in the CLASS', you know
      PE: Yeah
127. *L*: 'that's saying that I wanted to do SOMETHING ELSE' ??
128. but then WENT and FOUND OUT/I was about ONE hour off FIFTEEN
      PE: Right
      L: so.

Strophe 14
(Family and School)
Stanza 29
(Meaning of L's choice in his family)

Figure 5.1 Continued

129. *PE*: And that, HOW did,/I mean in TERMS of your FAMILY,
130. was it OK for YOU as a BOY
131. to CHOOSE to do something/that MOSTLY GIRLS DID?
    L: Yeah.
132. *PE*: That was ALL RIGHT?
    L: Yeah.

Stanza 30
('my sister': silence as support)
133. *PE*: And if it HADN'T have been ALL RIGHT,
134. HOW would you have FOUND OUT?
135. *L*: You know, it's, my SISTER/would have GONE ON ABOUT IT, you know.
136. *PE*: And she DIDN'T?
    L: No. (5 secs)

Strophe 15
(Jointly closing Q3)
Stanza 31
(L's summary: a return to the 'similar')
137. *PE*: Anything ELSE about being a BOY, in the FAMILY,/you'd like to say, from YOUR OWN family situation?
138. *L*: You know, I'd say we were BOTH/of SEXES in the FAMILY
139. were given the SAME AMOUNT of/RESPONSIBILITY and (3 secs) and CHOICE MAKING.
140. *PE*: Um. (6 secs). It sounds, sounds SURPRISINGLY EQUAL.
    L: Um.

Stanza 32
(PE's summary transition to Q4)
141. *PE*: That's INTERESTING, yeah.
142. And it sounds like THAT WORKED for YOU
143. and it WORKED for your SISTERS
    L: Um
    PE: to BE EQUAL?
144. Yeah. OK, mo, MOVING ON/from from THAT sort of THING
    (PE moves to question 4)

As indicated in the transcript, we have organised these 64 lines of Part 3 into 7 strophes comprised of 14 stanzas, generating a 'trail' of headlines as shown in Table 5.1.

Table 5.1 Outline of the narrative text L2/Q3 – Part 3

Part 3: A narrative of gendered schooling for the world of work (Lines 81–145)

Strophe 9: Co-constructing the narrative frame
  Stanza 19: PE recycles Q3 around the imperative 'ought'

Stanza 20: Lance shifts narrative frame from 'ought to become' to 'want' and 'try'

Strophe 10: Evaluating the narrative frame
Stanza 21: Lance contrasts 'should' with 'nice'
Stanza 22: Illustrating 'nice' – the covert 'ought' of independence and choice
Coda: 'that's what I mean by nice'

Strophe 11: Elaborating the theme of 'nice' in terms of choice
Stanza 23: Following the theme of choice – from abstraction to example
Stanza 24: Lance's narrative of supported choice – 'ask' not 'should' helps to distinguish 'wrong' from 'right' choices
Coda: Lance's 'options' choices guided through parental questioning

Strophe 12: Negotiating the theme of gender difference in relation to choice
Stanza 25: PE raises the theme of gender difference through questioning the 'similar' in Lance's family – Lance relocates this theme in terms of 'school is different'
Stanza 26: PE follows Lance who elaborates on gendered 'subjects'

Strophe 13: A different difference – Lance's negotiation of gendered 'subjects'
Stanza 27: What and how Lance chose
Stanza 28: Lance's narrative reflection on making his 'different' choice

Strophe 14: Family and school
Stanza 29: Meaning of Lance's choice in his family
Stanza 30: 'my sister' – silence as support

Strophe 15: Jointly closing Q3
Stanza 31: Lance's summary – a return to the 'similar'
Stanza 32: PE's summary transition to Q4

We have thus identified Part 3 as a jointly constructed narrative of gendered schooling for the world of work. An overview of our headlines suggests that across Part 3, Lance is engaged in a subtle and complex process of positioning and repositioning himself in relation to PE's recycling of Q3 at Stanza 19 and ways in which he follows this up. Lance shifts the narrative frame from PE's 'ought to become' to his preferred 'want' and 'try' (Stanza 20), indicating the point of this in evaluative terms of how choice rather than demand is 'nice' (Strophe 10). This frame is maintained across Strophe 11 with the addition that 'choice' may be helpfully interrogated, so that 'ask' rather than 'should' (i.e. being questioned by his parents about the reasons for his choices, rather than told what to choose) can help to distinguish 'wrong' from 'right' choices of school 'options'. In Strophe 12, PE introduces the theme of gender difference in relation to Lance's theme of 'choice' in his family. In response to this Lance makes a decisive discursive move from 'family' to his own gendered experience of how 'school is different' (Stanza 25), delineated in terms of gendered 'subjects'. Across Strophes 13 and 14 he then elaborates on his own active positioning in relation to these distinctions, first in terms of gendered implications of his making a 'different' choice at school, and then returning, in Strophe 15, to the perspective of 'choice' supported by his family. Broadly speaking, then, the headlines suggest a three-part structural organisation of this stretch of text: Strophes 9–11 addressed in the context of 'family'; Strophes 12–13 focused on 'school' and a narrative of gendered 'subjects' choices; and Strophes 14–15 refocused on 'family' and accomplishing closure of Q3 with transition to Q4.

Constructing the psychological subject: family, school and work

We have identified a three-part structural organisation of this stretch of text, starting with Strophes 9–11 addressed in the context of 'family'. The version of Q3 that Lance takes up across Strophe 9 carries forward PE's pitch glide emphasis on 'BOYS' and 'BECOME', only to disclaim and sideline (at this point) gender (l. 84), and to replace the researcher's imperious 'SHOULD' and 'OUGHT' with discourses of preference and choice, identified dynamically and discursively in terms of family relationships over time with 'MUM and DAD' (l. 85). He links the future orientation of 'BECOME' not with PE's retrospective 'LEARNED' but with 'a CASE' of how, by his parents' enquiring what 'you WANT to BECOME', he is encouraged to take up the responsibility to 'TRY' (ll. 84–7). Furthermore, triggering a structural move to Strophe 10, Lance first identifies this 'TRY/to BECOME' (l. 87) with the prospective world of 'WORK' (l. 90), and then with the present world of school, 'like DURING the OPTIONS' (l. 93). Both exemplify 'a CASE' (l. 86) he is making, in effect, for why he has reconstructed Q3 around 'WANT' rather than 'SHOULD', making an evaluative contrast negatively distinguishing 'NICE' from 'PESTERING' (ll. 91–2) and then positively defining 'what I mean by NICE' in terms of a family/ parental discourse of self-determination, 'THINK about it for yourSELF and/MAKE your OWN DECISIONS' (ll. 96–7).

This narrative positioning of himself in his family between the world of work and the world of school is repeated across Strophe 11. In response to his own on-line reflective questioning on PE's behalf about possible 'EXAMPLES' (l. 101) of choice-making, Lance returns to 'like DOING the OPTIONS again' (l. 102), elaborated through a rehearsal of acceptable questioning from his parents about how choices of options might 'HELP me get a JOB I WANTED' (ll. 104–6). These questions (see ll. 105, 106), however, differ from the preceding similar dramatisations (see ll. 86–7 and 96) in which Lance constructs himself as the object, 'you', of parental discourse. Instead, they are spoken in a kind of mixed parental alias requiring the grammatical inconsistency of represented parental speech *to* Lance which never-theless displaces the implied object 'you' with the narrating subject himself, *me* and *I*, thus constituting Lance's own voice speaking to himself. This flip-flop from object to subject suggests these questions are not so much (or simply) 'learned' or 'internalised' parental voices, as forms of reflexive questioning addressed by and to himself, signs, in effect, of practising something different from that problematic ascribed, hegemonic masculine identity, 'I'm ALWAYS/being TOLD ... / I HAVEN'T thought of the CONSEQUENCES of DOING something', which included 'the OFFENDING' (ll. 59–60). That is, Lance as a psychological subject of his own exemplary narrative (e.g. 'if I was THINKING ...', l. 103) validates and positions himself in a shared per-spective of the adult guidance of his parents 'to make SURE I CHOSE/in the RIGHT OPTIONS' (l. 108). Thus, across Strophes 9, 10 and 11, Lance locates or connects himself (a boy who has sexually abused a number of other children) in relation to a normative, taken-for-granted future orientation in which he effectively equates 'BECOME' with the adult world of 'WORK' mediated through school 'OPTIONS', and the potential disruptions and consequences of 'the OFFENDING' are, at this point, submerged.

From 'family' to 'school': renegotiating contexts of identity – a narrative of gendered 'subjects' and subject positions

Lance's shift in Strophe 9 from 'ought' to 'want' also elided PE's family focus on 'BOYS' (l. 83). In the second structural block of our Part 3 text (Strophes 12–14), when PE reintroduces this focus in Stanza 25 in terms of possible gender similarity/difference in the family in relation to choice (ll. 109–11), Lance uses PE's series of clumsy and closed interrogatives to offer three unemphasised 'Yeahs' (ll. 109, 110, 111) with no further elaboration. This politely and effectively disqualifies the context of PE's questions, providing instead for Lance's own specifically reflective and gendered refocusing on 'SCHOOL'. He achieves this shift by means of a skilful, rhetorical question (l. 112), which simultaneously changes the narrative context by treating the question as a truism with which he presumes PE agrees ('ISN'T IT'), but about which he has 'learned' and wants to tell PE something particular. Thus, this question triggers a focused narrative linking and differentiating his choices of school Options by means of which he accounts for his own subject positioning in relation to powerfully gender-stereotyped 'subjects'.

Lance introduces in relation to his narrative of Options, the gendered theme of negotiating 'SUBJECTS' (l. 116) choices in terms of constraints of canonical 'ought' and risks of personal 'want'. This, we will argue, extends and further situates him in relation to his account in Part 2 of gendered kinds of 'cleverness', particularly in relation to 'consequences'. Thus, analysis of Lance's narrative material in relation to school offers a significant context of '(s)tudying masculinity as a discursive practice' (Wetherell and Edley, 1998: 165). Connell (1995: 71), for instance, suggests that various sites can be identified which contribute to reproductive social processes of 'gender configuration'; one site he proposes includes 'institutions such as the state, the workplace and the school' (p. 73). He argues that such 'institutions are substantively, not just metaphorically, gendered' (ibid.). Similarly, Geertz (1997: 22) locates the school as a critical context in focusing attention on 'the individual's engagement with the established systems of shared meaning, with the beliefs, the values, and the understandings of those already in place in society as he or she is thrown in among them'. In particular, he points out the organising power of the 'classroom' in this process: 'It is there that mentality is most deliberately fashioned, subjectivity most systematically produced, and intersubjectivity – the ability to "read other minds" – most carefully nurtured' (p. 23). In, and in relation to, the world of school, particularly as it borders both on the family and on the world of work, Lance is clearly experimenting with and accomplishing gendered accounts and practices of subject positioning through the work of his narrative sense-making.

With Part 2 in mind, however, where Lance carefully elaborated on family gender differences in relation to 'the SCHOOL YEARS' (l. 47), how do we account for the apparent variability in his Part 3 account such that PE's questioning about Lance's 'SISTERS' (l. 109) in Stanza 25 generates no differences; a view which, we will notice, Lance returns to and confirms in closing Q3 (ll. 138–9)? The variability between the Part 2 account of connections for boys, privileging 'WANT' over the de-emphasised 'work', and the Part 3 account, emphasising connections between 'WANT to BECOME' and 'GO ROUND and TRY', suggest contextual differences in relation to which these 'cases' are doing different interactional work at different points during the interview. Whereas in Part 2, Lance develops a narrative negotiating, evaluating and situating himself as well as PE in relation to the canonical rumour that 'MEN are supposed to be MORE CLEVER' (l. 54), in Part 3 he is illustrating or defining through the choice of options what is 'NICE' about how his parents avoid telling their children what they 'SHOULD' choose, promoting instead their capacity for self-determination. The importance here of this contextual distinction is, we suggest, discursively demonstrated in that Lance's rhetorical shift from 'family' to 'school' (l. 112) provides him precisely with the occasion for a narrative account of exercising in his own right the family practice to 'THINK about it for yourSELF and/MAKE your OWN DECISIONS' (l. 96).

Building on his rhetorical question, which in effect serves as an Abstract for what follows, Lance accounts for how he has noticed 'SCHOOL is DIFFERENT' in terms of a gendered contrast of 'SUBJECTS': for sport the girls do 'NETBALL' (l. 116), for 'TECHNOLOGY' they do 'TEXTILES and FOOD' (l. 117); boys do 'RUGBY' (l. 116), and 'CDT and CRAFTS' (l. 117). The readiness of his delivery after a slight hesitation to begin with – 'You know, IT'S/sort of THINGS,/the SUBJECTS' (l. 116) – and clear-cut end of this particular fluency with our parallel 'Yeah' responses (l. 117), may indicate that these 'differences' did not take much reflection, are common knowledge, indeed stereotypical. At the same time, however, precisely by stating the obvious or the unremarkable Lance positions himself *reflexively*, as a kind of participant observer rather than submerged within the orbit of discursive and social practices that make up this school experience. That the gendered meanings of these 'SUBJECTS' should be so self-evident is not trivial, but rather is a measure of the power constraining individuals', including his own, choices of and participation in 'SUBJECTS' in relation to available social constructions of gendered identities. The obvious may in large part, therefore, constitute what Connell (1995: 73) means by suggesting that 'institutions are substantively, not just metaphorically, gendered'. The gendering of 'SUBJECTS' may be understood as exemplary in micro-terms, for instance, of how '(t)he state both institutionalises hegemonic masculinity and expends great energy in controlling it' (Connell, 1987: 128). To the extent that Lance's stereotyping observations could be trivialised they would also be 'invisiblised': naturalised and re-storied as unproblematic. To the extent, however, that they are constituted as significant, not simply in the abstract but, for instance, in relation to the discursive constructions of his experience in the immediate context of the interview, their articulation raises interpretive questions such as: So what?; What is the point of this plot?; Why has Lance made this particular connection at this point? That is, Lance's taken-for-granted observations raise questions about the interactional work they are doing, by means of which Lance is accounting for and situating himself. These interpretive questions, generated in response to Lance's initiation of this stretch of interview, help to draw analytic attention to the narrative function of his gendered stereotyping observations. We suggest that Lance's articulation of the 'SUBJECTS' stereotypes enables him to account for his own active subject positioning in relation to discourses and practices constituting the stereotypes in a way that neither abandons them nor sits comfortably with them. When PE asks 'Did you FOLLOW that kind of same PATTERN' (ll. 119), Lance unhesitatingly responds: 'NO, I DIDN'T actually, I went and done FOOD for TECHNOLOGY' (l. 120–1). He positions himself in terms of difference from, rather than choice between, the gender lines of stereotype he has just established. In terms, for instance, of the 'discursive practice' of masculinity this talk does not obviously constitute 'talking like a man' (Wetherell and Edley, 1998: 163). Rather, it serves Lance to position himself as a boy in a preferred relation to what he here identifies with 'GIRLS', just as previously he positioned himself in a preferred relation to his mother's/women's 'cleverness' in Part 2.

The Strophe 13 structural shift from Stanza 27 to Stanza 28 is marked in Lance's conversation by a move from, in effect (a) naming or identifying the institutional/canonical choices of gendered Options to (b) reflecting on his 'THINKING' (l. 125) at the time of his choosing. This discursive move constitutes an account as well as a demonstration of changed subject positioning. It involves Lance in accounting for how he took up a reflexive and evaluative position on his own social practice, not in relation to what Option he 'WANTED', but in relation to the relationship it puts him in with others, both girls and boys, and therefore also in relation to dominant discourses of gender attached to and articulated through the available 'SUBJECTS' and the social practices of his peers. In concrete, situational terms, Lance unfolds his narrative of choosing Options with rhetorical force and skill by means of a pitch glide emphasis in l. 125 that evinces a continuing present the more convincingly to recount and re-enact the very moment of his own on-the-spot reflection:

> 125 *L*: You know, but DURING the,/FILLING IN the/OPTIONS SHEET/I was STILL THINKING,/you know,
> 126 'I'M going to, /if I GO FOR THAT,/I'm going to be the ONLY BOY in the CLASS', you know
> *PE*: Yeah
> 127 *L*: 'that's saying that I wanted to do SOMETHING ELSE'.

In terms of narrative skill, this moment of delivery and moment of remembering represent a kind of 'high point' in the unfolding drama by means of which Lance situates PE, through intimately agentic particulars, in relation to his chosen theme of how 'SCHOOL is DIFFERENT.../for BOYS and GIRLS' (l. 112). He has identified available subject positions of 'SUBJECTS' in relation to dominant, institutionalised discourses of gender, positioned and accounted for himself as an 'active creator' (Wetherell and Edley, 1998: 168) of a particular, perhaps in his eyes unique, alternative masculine identity, and engaged reflexively on this positioning in terms of some of the possible real effects of this moment of social practice. How has he done this, and what is it all about?

To some extent in the above passage, Lance can be described as a 'hero' in his own story, standing up against dominant forces that dictate appropriate institutional choices and define the preordained, acceptably gendered subject position of, in this case, his masculine identity – he is both 'the *ONLY*' *and* 'the ONLY *BOY*'. He reflects on himself as a 'BOY' standing alone on a particular site of contestable ground, 'in the CLASS'. Lance accounts for the position or standpoint from which he 'was STILL THINKING' in gendered terms as a 'BOY', although, in his narrative, the gender-lines of 'SUBJECTS' have been drawn so that the choice he contemplates simultaneously disqualifies him from masculine identity and locates him with 'the GIRLS'. This dilemma raises questions about the meaning of the content of Lance's appropriation of the mantle of the word 'BOY'. It raises, in effect, a further problematic complexity: is what may be 'DIFFERENT' satisfactorily distinguished in terms of 'BOYS and GIRLS'? While the stereotypes suggest 'yes', Lance's 'THINKING' suggests 'no'. This thinking, as he recounts it, can itself in Lance's own terms be distinguished as 'female' since in this case (at least) he *is exercising* himself in thinking about 'CONSEQUENCES' (l. 59) in contrast to his ascribed problematic male identity of 'ALWAYS' not doing so (l. 59). His 'THINKING' teeters on the brink of entertaining a determinate consequence, 'I'M going to', and/or a possible consequence, 'if I GO'. In either case, for him 'to be the ONLY BOY in the CLASS...that's saying that I wanted to do SOMETHING ELSE', indicates not only a hypothetical consequence (e.g. what it might be like being in the future the only boy in a class of girls), but locates a much more immediate consequence muted in the de-emphasised delivery of the word 'saying' (l. 127). This word locates the narrative context of 'the CLASS' as the class in which he is considering the choice of 'SOMETHING ELSE', not the class he would be in if he chose 'SOMETHING ELSE'. It is in this rhetorically present, mixed 'CLASS' that Lance is 'STILL THINKING' of the consequences of his possible 'saying'; that is, in this case, this 'hero' is making sense of what it could mean for him to 'CHOOSE/what you WANTED' on the 'OPTIONS SHEET' (ll. 123–4) by way of the proposition 'THINK about it for yourSELF and/MAKE your OWN DECISIONS' (l. 96). In this case, however, the proposition generates a dilemma involving a complexity suggested by Connell's (1995) idea of 'hegemonic masculinity'.

'Hegemonic masculinity' Connell (1995: 77) suggests, 'can be defined as the configuration of gender practice which embodies the currently accepted answer to the problem of the legitimacy of patriarchy, which guarantees (or is taken to guarantee) the dominant position of men and subordination of women'. This explicitly historicised rendering of 'masculinity', consistent for instance with a feminist 'aim ... to *relativise* masculinity and men's claims to authority in all domains' (Wetherell and Edley, 1998: 156), supports the observation that '(h)egemony...is a historically mobile relation' (ibid.) and 'does not mean total control' (Connell, 1995: 37). Thus, although it can be said that 'the main axis of the power-structure of gender is the general connection of authority with masculinity' (Connell, 1987: 109), this clearly can be contested or 'disrupted' (Connell, 1995: 37). Lance is to some degree discursively situating himself as locally 'disrupting' this power structure by way of preferring certain kinds of gendered 'cleverness' and considering Options that betray perceived gender stereotypes of subjects, as well as reflexively situating himself to consider effects on his masculine identity in his relations with others 'in the CLASS'.

However, the distinction of the 'DIFFERENT' between 'BOYS and GIRLS', as Lance appears to put it in relation to the gendered institutional context of school, falls short of a more inclusive, complex understanding of hegemonic masculinity which his own further 'THINKING' may suggest. Lance's 'THINKING' about being 'the ONLY BOY in the CLASS ... that's saying I wanted to do SOMETHING ELSE' (l. 127) suggests not only a 'standing alone' in his 'saying' as a 'BOY' in a class of 'GIRLS', but also 'standing apart' as a 'BOY' from other 'BOYS' in the class who, whatever (or whether) they may be 'THINKING' for themselves, may neither be 'saying' or deciding they want 'to do SOMETHING ELSE' that transgresses the hegemonic discourses and practices that constitute and enforce gender lines. It is not possible in the context of our Q3 text to extend this analysis, for example, as Edley and Wetherell (1997: 202) have done, to warrant an 'action orientation of different constructions of identity', to interpret from this portion of the interview, for instance, to what extent Lance's narrative may indicate 'resistance' or 'complicity' (ibid.) in relation to the 'legitimacy of patriarchy' or '*relations* between the different kinds of masculinity' (Connell, 1995: 37). However, what the text does suggest through this narrative of gendered choice is the fundamental importance of narrative itself as a discursive practice employed by Lance, through and by means of which he can be heard to be actively engaged in making sense of himself as a boy in relation to dominant discourses and social practices constitutive of available institutionalised subject positions of girls but also of other boys.

Lance's account, situating himself as 'the ONLY BOY', teeters, as we have put it, not only on the edge of 'THINKING' about certain consequences, but also on the edge of what Connell (1995: 77) describes as 'practices and relations that construct the main patterns of masculinity in the current Western gender order', including hegemony, subordination, complicity and marginalisation. Although his

narrative remains in the realm of 'STILL THINKING', neither achiev-
ing 'saying' nor in the event a choice at all (as we will indicate
below), it nevertheless accomplishes interactional work between
himself and PE. Through this account Lance clearly situates himself
as 'THINKING' *on the margins* of the dominant discourses he reflects
on. While we do not suggest that thinking on the margins and 'marginalisation' are equivalent, Connell's (1995: 81) understanding of
'marginalisation', that it is 'always relative to the *authorisation* of the
hegemonic masculinity of the dominant group', is useful in drawing
attention to possible and textually anchored meanings in Lance's
narrative account. This *'authorisation'* powerfully legitimates the
dominant dimorphic distinction organising gendered 'SUBJECTS'
and reinforcing traditional gendered subject positions, making a
'classroom' contribution to 'the individual's engagement with established systems of shared meanings' (Geertz, 1997: 22). It enforces and
reproduces, that is, a particular hegemonic masculinity of the dominant group. What it does *not* do, certainly in Lance's account of his
lived and reflected-upon experience here, is extend itself to the kinds
of cleverness he shows a definite yet ambivalent preference and
desire for in Part 2 (e.g. 'I ALWAYS/WANTED TO BE able to PLAN
things out ... like GOOD DETAIL', ll. 70–1), or the kinds of Options
he as a 'BOY' might want to choose. For these, he receives *no 'authorisation'* and, in this sense, is 'decentred' from the 'main axis of the
power-structure of gender' which, Connell (1995: 37) suggests, 'is the
general connection of authority with masculinity'.

The extent to which Lance situates himself in relation to and
through these preferences may constitute a significant degree of
principled, if ambivalent and unstable, 'marginalisation' not simply
in terms of being 'the ONLY BOY' amongst 'the GIRLS', but 'the
ONLY BOY' wanting and thus accounting for himself in terms of
'SOMETHING ELSE' amongst 'the BOYS'. Perhaps for the same kinds
of reasons that Lance may choose to discursively accomplish a view
of himself as 'hero' in his own narrative, this view in practice may
threaten to fill the word 'ONLY' with consequences of relational exclu-
sion and isolation signifying unshared and/or largely problematical
discourses of masculine identities. These in turn may drain the word
'BOY' of available, acceptable and accepted meanings, thus reconsti-
tuting the 'hero' in the discursive and social practices of his subject
positioning not as standing his ground but in a kind of 'free-fall',

experiencing what Connell (1995: 137) describes as 'a kind of gender vertigo' that has yet not fully, but perhaps has to an 'experimental' extent, impelled him 'to reach for other ways of structuring the world'. Here, for example, 'saying' (l. 127) may understandably remain de-emphasised, muted, precisely because to 'SAY' would make Lance visibly accountable for what 'STILL THINKING' keeps implicit and to some extent therefore allows him to hold open, unde-cided and legitimately secret.

Co-constructing narrative closure: a performance of identities

PE returns the interview to 'family' (Stanza 29), and Lance states (Stanza 30) that the indicator of any disapproval of his possible choice of Options would have been that 'my SISTER would have GONE ON ABOUT IT' (l. 135). His following firm 'No' and 5-second silence suggests he has no more to say about this. Instead, in response to PE's last recycling of Q3 at l. 137, Lance expresses as a considered opinion an evaluation of his 'family' experience around 'RESPONSIBILITY and ... CHOICE MAKING' (ll. 138–9). The themes of this across Part 3 have supported a family preference for self-determination, consti-tuted 'what I mean by NICE' (ll. 96–7), been situated in relation to both the worlds of school and work, and been dramatised through his narrative account of choices of subjects carrying implications for his own gendered subject positioning. In effect, Lance has not only told a narrative *about* a central family discourse and relational prac-tice, he has *performed* it through its co-constructed telling, at which he has shown himself to be highly adept. Part of this includes his ability to decide when he has said enough. Thus, with his mind on 'MOVING ON' (l. 144), PE takes his own 6-second pause and Lance's immobile 'Ums' (ll. 140 and 143) as cues to embark on Q4.

Across Q3 Lance can be seen to be negotiating, balancing and eval-uating his narrative practices around 'RESPONSIBILITY and CHOICE MAKING' with particular implications around gendered identities. These implications, we suggest, are confronted in terms of two par-ticularly significant dilemmas raised through Q3, neither of which is resolved or established in terms of Lance situating or accounting for himself in some definitive way. The first involves the dilemma of an unreflective male cleverness associated, albeit tangentially, with 'the OFFENDING' as typical rather than atypical of 'ANYTHING' he does.

The second involves the dilemma of the 'ONLY BOY', of what discourses and what subject positions are available (or not) for making
sense of choices that might precipitate 'gender vertigo'. Each of these
dilemmas, we suggest, is rooted and embedded in his lived experience, in those family and institutional discourses and practices by
means of which he situates himself 'AS A BOY' through stories he
tells about himself and stories he tells that others tell about him.
These include 'the OFFENDING' as well as 'a bigger picture in (his)
own words of how (he sees himself) growing up into a young man'.
The interactional work Lance's concluding statement performs at this
point is to draw PE's attention to how he has been practising through
the interview conversation to make sense of himself in relation to
the overarching thematic focus of Q3 in such a way that certain gendered dilemmas and resources around 'RESPONSIBILITY and
CHOICE MAKING' are highlighted. These gendered dilemmas and
resources are storied and interactional, located neither 'in' nor 'separate' from himself, but through those discursive practices by means
of which he situates and accounts for himself in relation simultaneously to the real time of the interview and to the canonical as well as
personal narrative versions of his own lived time, past, present and
future and possible identities.

The intertexuality of interview narrative and both canonical and alternative cultural narratives

Bruner (1987: 14) argues that 'life narratives' or 'autobiographical
accounts (even the ones we tell ourselves) (are) notably unstable',
thus making 'life stories highly susceptible to cultural, interpersonal,
and linguistic influences'. He suggests that over time, however, 'we
become the autobiographical narratives by which we "tell about" our
lives', becoming to some degree 'variants of the culture's canonical
forms' (p. 15). Although Lance's narratives are not, and were not
elicited as, 'autobiographical' in Bruner's sense, nevertheless through
the processes of narrative analysis it is clear that, even in the context
of the interview understood as jointly produced, his personal narrative
sense-making reflects the impact of, as well as choices he is making
in relation to, canonical narratives and organising social discourses.
He is an active participant in accounting for and situating himself in
relation to what Bruner (1987) calls 'possible lives' that are part of

one's culture, whether these are thought of, for instance, in terms of hegemonic or of marginalised masculine identities.

Researching from a feminist perspective highlights amongst other things the problematising and relativising of traditional masculinity as a dominant narrative model constitutive in highly constraining ways of alternative narratives of gendered 'possible lives'. As Gergen and Gergen (1993: 193) argue: '(t)o the extent that narratives are gendered, furnishing different structures of meaning for men as opposed to women, so do they contribute to cultural patterns that differentiate between the genders and prescribe both what is likely and unlikely during a lifetime'. But, as Edley and Wetherell (1997: 204) state, for instance: 'The meanings given to masculinities are not static or unitary' and the '*contested* nature of masculinity over time' appears to be the 'rule', rather than the 'myth' of naturalised transhistorical hegemonic masculinity. Connell's (1995: 84) work historicising masculinities suggests that it has become possible to 'logically speak of the crisis of a gender order as a whole, and of its tendencies towards crisis'. Evidence of this 'crisis', he argues, its signs of change, is, however, 'not the crumbling of the material and institutional structures of patriarchy', but '(w)hat has crumbled, in the industrial countries, is the '*legitimation* of patriarchy' (p. 226). This suggestion specifically problematises the traditional assumptions and practices revolving around 'the main axis of the power structure of gender' which, Connell (1987: 109) argues, 'is the general connection of authority with masculinity'. While, for instance, Lance's perspective on the institutional structures sustaining gendered school Options choices suggests little of 'patriarchy' has 'crumbled' there, nevertheless, his narrative of his own wants and choices in school, clearly anchored in various ways in his family experience, moves him to reflect on and evaluate possible real effects in his own life and relationships of 'saying' what could situate him as 'the ONLY BOY in the class'. That is, while the 'structures', including their expectations and constraints, clearly stand, nevertheless Lance, negotiating gendered identity on the margins of canonical gendered narratives, at least *entertains* alternative subject positioning which does not sit uncritically with a traditional, unquestioned '*legitimation* of patriarchy'.

Within the perspectives of our thematic interpretation of Q3, we suggest that it can be clearly said of Lance's narrative material that 'culture "speaks itself" through an individual's story' (Riessman, 1993: 5).

At the same time, it is also clear that Lance sees himself, and wants PE to see him too, as actively engaged in evaluating, choosing and reflecting upon a range of cultural givens (discourses and practices) mediated through his parents, school and the awaiting world of work. A measure of his agency is precisely evident through narrative analysis 'highlighting the remarkable subtleness and sophistication of (his) talk and its *designed* features' (Edley and Wetherell, 1997: 205). Furthermore, part of this 'agentic' negotiating of dominant discourses and available subject positions, is the more radical possibility of forays into negotiating 'replacement' discourses and alternative subject positions. We have suggested above that Lance's sense-making, in some ways on the margins of dominant discourses and gendered identity expectations, can be seen to entertain, for instance, a preferred kind of 'female' 'cleverness' which he himself reflexively contrasts with a 'masculine' 'cleverness' typified by not thinking 'of the CONSEQUENCES of DOING something', including 'the OFFENDING' (ll. 59–60).

To the extent that thematic interpretation has privileged and warranted at least an awareness of this kind of 'marginal' activity, we have suggested it may also serve to link the validation of personal narrative analysis with contemporary 'alternative' therapeutic approaches which, for instance, focusing on the discursive and social practices of people's 'constructed meaning...by which they define and promote themselves', seek to find and/or to generate 'narratives that promote a difference in the way people experience and act in their situations' (Saleebey, 1994: 357). This view, effectively assuming that 'people are simultaneously the products *and* the producers of discourse', both 'constrained and enabled by language' (Edley and Wetherell, 1997: 206), is likely to privilege the kinds of discursive and narrative means by which, for instance, Lance is actively engaged in making sense of himself to himself and (in this case) through the research interviews to PE. That is, for example, part of the utility of narrative analysis with our particular interview material, is that it is methodologically able to attend to precisely the stories and sense-making which dominant formulations of sexually abusing boys typically individualise, pathologise and subordinate.

Connell (1995: 72), arguing that 'when we speak of masculinity and femininity we are naming configurations of gender practice', proposes the idea of '*gender projects*': 'These are processes of configuring practice through time, which transform their starting-points in gender structure.' A critical narrative point in this analysis of 'lives' in terms of gender projects and 'the social reproduction of hegemonic masculinity' is what Connell describes as 'the *moment of engagement* with hegemonic masculinity' (p. 122). This is 'the moment in which the boy takes up the project of hegemonic masculinity as his own'; it is a 'moment' of 'appropriation' (ibid.). While the analysis above of Lance's Q3 differs significantly from the methods of life narrative analysis employed by Connell, the idea of 'a moment of engagement' has, we suggest, a useful bearing on our critical narrative analytic approach. Connell's use of the word 'moment' indicates a historicising temporality; it indicates social, including discursive, practices through a particular period of time by means of which a boy's 'appropriation' of the 'project of hegemonic masculinity' is performed or accomplished. The fine-grained analysis and thematic interpretation of Lance's personal narratives, jointly constructed through the real time of the Q3 research interview, offers, we suggest, some understanding of what (textually anchored in Lance's own words and his points of view) may be described as some of his 'starting-points in gender structure'. These, we have tried to show, involve Lance in normative and possibly alternative reflections on constitutive gendered discourses and practices of family life and organisation, parenting, school and expectations of the world of work.

While, certainly from a feminist perspective (e.g. MacLeod and Saraga, 1988), Lance as a boy who has sexually abused other children, exemplifies rather than deviates from normative, dominant 'power-based behaviours or thoughts', he at the same time can be seen positioning himself, negotiating and performing a view of himself which does not sit uncritically with the 'appropriation' of hegemonic masculinity but may even represent certain means for keeping open and unresolved that culturally normative '*moment of engagement*'. At least, it appears that 'the plural rather than unitary character of (this boy's) experiences' (Wetherell and Edley, 1998: 159) includes or has generated the inclusion of simultaneous and contradictory discourses and subject positions, both hegemonic and abusive (linked by Lance himself to 'the OFFENDING'), and to some extent reflexively narrated and entertaining alternative and perhaps counterhegemonic possibilities. For example, in linking 'the OFFENDING' as part of 'ANYTHING' with a masculine cleverness that fails to consider consequences to 'DOING something', Lance situates himself in relation to his own sexual offending as *potentially* taking responsibility to critically evaluate his 'power-based behaviours or thoughts'; and, in linking his mother's preferred cleverness with what 'I ALWAYS WANTED TO BE' (l. 70), he may *potentially* be situating himself in relation to a preferred nonabusing future.

The point of these comments, of course, is not to suggest that the above thematic analysis 'proves' what Lance may or may not 'WANT to BECOME' (l. 86), either in relation to his sexually abusing behaviour or any other aspects of his life. What it does suggest is that Lance's personal narrative material is rich both with signs of multiple, contesting and constitutive canonical discourses and with signs of his actively practising to situate and account for himself in relation and in counter-relation to these. It suggests a potential instability and ambivalence in how Lance negotiates choices amongst, and articulates accounts through, these discourses and identities 'as a BOY'. On the one hand these leave him 'highly susceptible to cultural, interpersonal, and linguistic influences' (Bruner, 1987: 14) and pursuing a 'gender project' involving sexual abuse, but on the other they may be preventing engagement with hegemonic masculinity and, instead, mobilising possible alternative discourses and subject positions of masculinity. A narrative analytic approach, we are suggesting, privileges and raises questions and possibilities *from within and through Lance's personal narrative material and sense-making practices*. It provides some 'windows' not only onto ways this boy may be situating himself in relation to canonical narratives constitutive of the culturally incited and simultaneously prohibited 'possible life' of male sexual abusing, but also onto discourses and social practices in which he already shows significant investment and skill and which could perhaps constitute an empowering basis for learning to 'LOVE' to become effective 'to SOLVE (his) OWN' problems.

Nevertheless, the story of his ascribed problematic identity – 'I'm ALWAYS/being TOLD, you know,/not, I HAVEN'T thought of the/ CONSEQUENCES of DOING something' (l. 59) – is not only overtly linked by Lance to 'the OFFENDING' (l. 60) and thus implicated with dangerous masculinity, but its contrasting story of thinking and planning ahead (characterised by his mother) is also characteristically linked to 'grooming' which would be virtually impossible without precisely this kind of cleverness. Thus, a further dilemma for

Lance in relation to dangerous masculinity may be that, as not all men's (e.g. his father's) behaviour, which may typically not consider consequences, is necessarily abusive, so all women's (e.g. his mother's) thinking/planning, which may consider consequences, is, in the hands of men, not automatically nonabusive. However, it may be consistent with Lance's view that although the construction of masculine identities that include thinking 'of the/CONSEQUENCES of DOING something' does not necessarily constitute taking responsibility for avoiding abuse, the real effects of this construction in his life may make available subject positions more capable of reflexive accountability.

6
Claims and Counterclaims: Working Critically with Narratives

Aims: to encourage movement from illustrating our approach to critical narrative analysis to engaging readers in practice with other narrative texts and contexts

In this chapter we hope, by a systematic review of key theoretical, methodological and related issues around our illustrative engagement with one boy's narrative material, to encourage readers to try for themselves investigations using 'inclusive strategies' of narrative analysis – studies of 'how narratives work and the work they do' (Mishler, 1995: 17) – and contribute to the generation of situated and warrantable *psychosocial* 'knowledge' from a critical perspective. In the interests of brevity we will be very sparing on references assuming our review will help readers relocate on a chapter-by-chapter basis particular issues and themes they may want to return to. As we have noted, the close-up work of detailed and extended analysis, particularly taking into account both the 'messiness' of how personal narratives are *said* and the complex contexts of their joint-production, can be daunting and confusing. This may in part explain a typical preference for working rather uncritically with de-contextualised 'snippets' whilst embracing ascriptive interpretations. With this in mind, it seems appropriate to organise a summary of our theoretical and methodological claims simply on a chapter-by-chapter basis, thus creating a kind of step-by-step overview that at the same time reflexively reviews the overall interactional work of our discussion. We will do this under two general headings: approach and application.

Claims relating to *approach* draw attention to the inseparability of theory and method, in particular to how in our case the choice to situate the field of our research interest, sexually abusing boys, in relation to feminist and social constructionist theory, suggested the possible utility of employing discursive methodologies with this 'clinical population'. Broadly, our argument in this regard is that this theoretical approach to, or critical reframing of, the dominant field privileges the use of qualitative methodologies (specifically, discourse and narrative analyses) capable of generating different psychosocial 'knowledges' with different implications for research and practice. Claims relating to *application*, constituting the body of our illustrative analysis, are reviewed step-by-step in relation to how in each chapter we engage with our texts in increasingly complex and extended ways. Some suggestions for readers will also be offered to help bridge the movement from demonstration to taking up invitations to further practice in their own way. Certain theoretical and methodological questions that arise out of this process of reviewing will be carried forward for discussion under Counterclaims and Contestations.

The aim here will not be to lay to rest every possible objection to discourse or narrative analysis, but simply to recognise that debates and dialogues continue where the paradigm shift from *the* framework to *a* framework (Stivers, 1993) has been recognised in the social sciences, thus supporting both a more inclusive attitude to methodologies and greater professional accountability with regard to informing theoretical and value assumptions.

Approach

Broadly, in Chapter 1, we situate our proposal for a critical narrative analysis in the historicised context of emerging *psychosocial studies*, in which amongst other changes traditional psychological assumptions about 'a bounded human subject' are made problematic and, instead, attention is given to the social construction of 'the psychosocial subject'. We have included for this paperback edition a range of up-dated references positioning the book in relation to developing debates affecting both narrative theory and methods, and, to some extent, aspects of the field of sexually abusing boys/young men. We argue that because psychosocial research of this kind is part of the enterprise of examining the conditions for knowledge out of which disciplinary power arises, it offers critical leverage on psychological theories and practices. We suggest that a critical stance becomes especially significant because of the contribution psychology itself makes to the construction of its own subject; that is, its claims to knowledge are themselves exertions of power. From this reflexive position, we argue that qualitative methods particularly serve the kinds of interpretive work or attention to meaning-making and investments in positioning (professional as well as in everyday life) given priority in psychosocial studies. A key point here is that qualitative research is linked with a paradigmatic revolution affecting the social and psychological sciences, which has contributed to the erosion of the hegemony of traditional empirical science in determining what counts as knowledge. This includes advocacy of a constructionist rather than representational paradigm for understanding language, so that research becomes concerned with gathering and analysing discursive forms, talk and text, and with how dominant discourses or canonical narratives and related issues of power and other social practices, may constitute available identities or subject positions and prevent or marginalise others. This enables us to privilege individuals' sense-making in their own words and from their own points of view, without losing sight of social contexts and responsibility.

In this way, agency may be placed in the foreground for analysis in relation to choices in, and accountability for, the discursive, performative distribution of subject positions, while at the same time interrogating the constitutive power of dominant discourses. The view that what counts as 'knowledge' is not neutral but is ideologically invested, and that the social construction of meaning is thus closely allied with power, has served feminists in the deconstruction of gender relations and relativising of masculinity as a socially constructed 'version of subjectivity' (Wetherell, 1992: 4–5). In this broad theoretical context, we link our interest in 'the *psychosocial* subject' with the methodological resources of narrative analysis. We suggest that its capacity for close attention to the social construction of subjectivities in relation to dominant discourses, and its potential for reflexive openness, make narrative analysis a specific discourse methodology capable of

cortical
narrative

critically contributing to the interplay between personal and social change. We argue that personal narratives, typically emerging around people's experiences of breaches between ideal and real, self and society, may have special importance for the narrator as well as for critical research. The alternatives of constructing coherence in the face of such breaches or constructing ways for keeping the coherence of the narrated event open to question and preventing foreclosure, both have implications for personal meaning-making. Furthermore, the ways people talk have material effects in terms of subject positions and fitting or not fitting in with dominant forms of social life.

We commence our approach to critical narrative analysis, therefore, emphasising that making overt the *inseparability of theory and method* is part and parcel not only of accounting for researcher investment and choices of investigative approach, that is, of meeting the demand for 'reflexive engagement around professional assumptions and positionings' (Frosh and Emerson, 2005: 321), but also of a reflexive acknowledgement of broader debates suggesting that what is going on is a struggle between different ways of conceptualising psychology and the social sciences, rather than simply the best strategies of experiment and investigation. While the specific development and content of our field of research interest (sexual abusiveness) need not be reviewed here (see Emerson and Frosh, 2001), what can be summarised to exemplify this reciprocal situating of the theoretical and methodological includes in our case: (a) that a feminist perspective making masculinity problematic is significant for retheorising sexual abuse with particular reference to boys who sexually abuse other children; (b) that the professional field of sexual abuse, firmly anchored in assumptions of traditional empirical science, can both be challenged and reframed by feminist and social constructionist theory; (c) that this retheorising of the field, with its discursive orientation and 'turn to text', invites applications of qualitative methodologies attuned to subjective meaning-making, including, in particular, (d) discourse and narrative analytic approaches sensitive to how abusive articulations of masculine identities may be both constituted and chosen in relation to dominant discourses and social practices of gender and power. Furthermore, central to these claims is that agency, for instance a boy's accounts of and personal responsibility for sexual abusing, is not compromised through the process of retheorisation, nor is it reduced to deviance and pathology.

Rather, agency is interrogated and recentralised in relation both to social accountability for changing prevailing normative discourses, and to personal accountability for choices and for alternative subject positions of nonabusive masculine identities.

On the basis of these positional claims, we engage in presenting a critical approach to narrative analysis of extended texts. We demonstrate the methodological potential and substantive value of an increasingly thickly warranted analysis capable of generating new ways of 'hearing' and professional sense-making in relation to our research participant's own 'ideas, thoughts, memories in (his) own words' (Reinharz, 1992: 19) as articulated in our research interviews. In terms of the possible 'utility' of such an approach, our aim is not to polarise in relation to dominant empirical research traditions, but rather to support the generation of different questions and different understandings as legitimate, practical and challenging *psychosocial* contributions to, in this case, a rapidly developing field the canonical narratives of which may be critically viewed as not so much on the brink of consolidation (e.g. Ryan and Lane, 1997: 198–9) as of transformation.

Application

Our aim, expressed in Chapter 1, is to demonstrate an approach to critical narrative analysis emphasising reflexive attention to 'fit', in the sense of constraints and developmental possibilities, between theory, method and application, that makes 'doable' contextualised, close narrative analysis over extended stretches of textual material. The illustrative choice of 'clinical' focus (sexually abusing boys), analysing portions of one boy's interview material, is purposefully situated with this 'fit' in mind. We propose a continuing dual focus in the analysis of the texts, concentrating on the participant's discursive and narrative resources while at the same time maintaining a perspective of both personal responsibility and social accountability for choices that sustain, challenge and potentially reformulate discourses constitutive of available subject positions. A principal analytical claim evident through the examples of textual analysis across Chapters 2, 3, 4 and 5, is that approaching our participant Lance in ways that privilege and thus make more room for his personal narrative accounts, also makes more available the kinds of textual material that can contribute to understanding in his own words and from his own point of view how he makes sense of himself and his behaviour, and what kinds of social discourses, beliefs and assumptions may serve to organise and sustain these accounts. Thus, in these chapters we both demonstrate and seek to warrant the argument that personal narratives can offer a critical window on processes of social construction of (here, specifically, gendered) identity. In relation to sexual abuse these narratives, on the one hand, continue to sustain traditionally dominant versions of masculinity, but, on the other hand, they also show signs of or resources for counterhegemonic struggle with, and resistance or alternatives to, a boy's apprenticeship to discourses of abusive masculinity. Our review of *application*, anchored theoretically as we have indicated, summarises in a step-by-step fashion how we develop and apply critical narrative analysis, followed by some further suggestions for 'getting started' with analytic entry into other narrative texts and contexts.

The unit of personal narrative analysis

In Chapter 2, we raise by way of example, and then address in terms of the issue of the *'unit of analysis'*, a reflexive question designed to *evaluate the quality and availability of our narrative material* (drawn, in this case, from Lance's offence-specific interview): whether the interviewer's questions were eliciting what Lance wanted him to hear, and whether this was what the researchers wanted to analyse. We examine this in principle around the first question of the first semistructured interview with Lance (Q1). We point out in Chapter 1 that our Interview Guide was designed to elicit personal narrative material. Reflecting both issues germane to the field of our research and our theoretical frameworks, the Guide was therefore constructed of 'open' questions as triggers for an interview process intended to be more like a 'collaborative conversation' than like an assessment or interrogation. We propose that a reflexive evaluation of our questions must not only recognise the privileging of the boy's control over his own words, but do so in such a way that his words and meaning-making can be interrogated and premature closure around assumptions of gender and power (e.g. socially sanctioned power-based behaviours) resisted. We situate and develop this response illustratively in relation to aspects of narrative theory bearing on methodological issues of *transcription and interpretation*, which in practice become significant from the first stab at relistening to produce a raw text. Discussing the first question of the first interview with Lance, we point out its intention to privilege Lance's sense-making rather than inventorying his sexually abusive behaviours, and suggest that across the text of Q1 he stays focused on meaning-making responses to the question, developing these through a series of personal narratives generated around a number of identifiable themes.

We observe the early importance for our analysis of the dawning *recognition in practice of the joint-production of meaning*, of coming to see the interview conversation as the context for the construction of meaning, rather than a vehicle for simply carrying or representing prefabricated formulations of meaning, the interviewer's own (e.g. the interview questions) or the respondent's. We point out that this facilitated PE's early recognition of the emergence of personal narratives not in typical textbook paragraphs but through the to and fro, in effect the 'messiness', of highly idiosyncratic discourse grammar. Focusing on the activity of *transcription as itself inevitably interpretive*, as theory and value driven, we underline reflexive attention to *researcher accountability for the perspectival or situated production of knowledge*. Thus, we re-emphasise links between theory (in our work, feminist and social constructionist orientations) and methodological choices (in our case, a preference for transcription that both reflects the joint-production involved in the emergence of personal narratives during the interview and enables those interactions to be an integral part of the narrative analysis).

With these preliminary ideas in mind, we then illustrate, first, our response to determining where a personal narrative segment begins and ends; second, how two different approaches to reducing narrative text bring forth different kinds of interpretive emphases; then, third, follow these with an example recommending for our purposes transcription reflecting the emergence and interpretation of personal narrative as jointly produced. So, first, in identifying the emergence of Lance's personal narrative, we argue that although identifiable as a relatively discrete unit, much of its meaning depends on where it is situated in the thematic development of the interview conversation. Focusing initially on the *narrative as a unit*, we reduce the text to a *core narrative* organised in terms of Labov's (Riessman, 1993: 59) structural categories. This approach tends to treat an understanding

of any particular text as the logical development of a position statement. Second, we introduce conventions for narrative transcriptions
as developed by Gee (1991), who suggests the *internal discourse structure of texts provides 'cues'* for how the teller invites interpretation. We
link this narrative methodology, and our preferences for it, to Edley
and Wetherell's (1997) characterisation of 'bottom up' in contrast to
'top down' approaches to discursive research. Gee's (1991) attention
to cues anchored in how a text is *said*, supports the exercise of *analytic restraints on relativism in relation to possible acceptable interpretations*. Thus, analysis of the same stretch of Lance's Q1 text using Gee's
transcription draws interpretive attention to a tentativeness and
impulsiveness in his speaking suggesting very different affective
investment in the telling of this narrative from its reading as a kind
of position statement.

Third, recognising that *different sense-making is privileged by different
transcriptions*, we relocate and analyse the same stretch of Lance's Q1
text transcribed to reflect its joint-production (although, not at this
point, fully using Gee's notation). We argue that analysis of the text
as jointly produced allows for examination of 'power relations in the
production of personal narrative' (Riessman, 1993: 20). This can help
to resist textual appropriation by offering some potential for absent
narrators to retain the kinds of control over their own words and
meanings that they exercise in the real time of the interview through
their moment-by-moment choices of how to respond and to situate
themselves. This analysis draws attention to the pace of a process of
*foregrounding and backgrounding in the discursive development and
mutual contextualising of various themes* through which it becomes
possible to see Lance not only *telling a story* but, through his *telling*,
to be *working to accomplish interpretive control* over how he wants PE
to understand him. For example, our analysis suggests that while PE
held on to thematic material introduced by Lance in the word
'wrong', in particular pursuing a question around the origins of his
moral understanding, he can be seen to miss a significant cue indicating a wider thematic contextualising of 'wrong' in terms of
'desire', identifying this narrative as embedded or nested in a longer
more complex stretch of Lance's narrative meaning-making. We
argue that Lance links his personal 'desire' for what he evaluates as
'wrong' to a normative discourse of 'secrecy' which, however, he
appears also to evaluate as 'wrong'. Similarly, we suggest his account

of 'desire' draws on the dominant 'male sex drive' discourse (Hollway, 1989: 54) that, nevertheless, does not resolve the dilemmas of his narrative. Overall, we argue from the text that while these dominant discourses serve to orient PE towards, and to support, Lance's aims, actions and evaluations, they emerge interactively across the complex process of our jointly produced interview focused around Q1. We conclude, in relation to the reflexive question raised at the beginning of this chapter, (a) that in response to Q1 Lance has been able to tell PE what he wants him to hear, in his own words and in his own way, (b) that at the same time the focus of this stretch of interview remains on the kinds of questions and interests brought to the research by the researchers, that is, (c) discourse around the research question constitutes our critical unit of analysis, in the exploration of which, (d) narrative analysis is an appropriate methodology.

The severity of the requirement for close transcription and monitoring of the interactive aspects of the research interview may make this approach less immediately appealing than more global methods of qualitative research such as thematic or content analysis. However, our suggestion is that theoretical and practical advantages flow relatively quickly from the attention paid to basic questions concerning the structuring of texts and the ways in which narratives, both fragmentary and more complete, arise out of interactive processes. For example, the search for 'stories' in a text is inherently problematic, as it implies the imposition of an uncertain but pre-given framework (what makes up a 'story'?) to the idiosyncrasies of an individual speaker's attempt to articulate her or his experiences. Whilst there continue to be presuppositions in our approach – for instance that stressed and emotionally marked elements in texts indicate issues of significance for the speaker, or that the work surrounding 'breaches' in narrative warrants especially close attention – there is much more room for reconsidering what might be meant by a 'narrative' or 'story' in any individual case. Exploring unclear fragments, offering a 'history' of the emergence of particular stories out of the engagement of interviewer and interviewee with one another, attending to the rhetorical demands and consequences of particular speech acts: these possibilities arise out of the closely grounded examination of what has been said and how. In so doing, critical narrative analysis constantly subverts tendencies to assume that the 'meaning' of any utterance can be understood on a priori grounds, rather than as embedded in, and emergent from, its very specific narrative context. For qualitative researchers, the discipline of this perspective therefore acts as a philosophically congruent constraint on wild imagination as well as on pre-emptive expert interpretive strategies.

Linguistic tools and interpretive levels

In Chapter 3, we begin to demonstrate an extended narrative analysis carried forward across Chapters 4 and 5, structured and developed around three Parts of Lance's response to the third question in the second, non-offence related interview (L2/Q3). Building on the understanding that transcription itself is an interpretive process driven or organised by theory (exemplified in Chapter 2), and that different approaches reflect and serve different purposes, here we expand on our preliminary explanations of Gee's (1991) methodology, illustrating in some detail each of his five linguistic structural levels of narrative analysis, with a view to demonstrating thematic interpretation of L2/Q3 and with increasing attention to the interview as discourse (Mishler, 1986). Overall, we argue that *narrative analysis offers important 'windows' onto an arena of textual interactions*, including potential contestations, between the micro-moves of Lance's active, multiple and discursive subject positionings and the constitutive presence of canonical narratives which constrain possibilities for articulating, let alone developing, 'replacement discourses' and alternative subject positions of masculine identity. We demonstrate that looking at longer texts facilitates, rather than makes daunting or unwieldy, their analysis in terms of interactional processes, in terms of voices in context rather than disconnected responses to disembodied questions. With utility in mind, we also suggest from our own worked example that this kind of analysis supports approaches to therapeutic work with sexually abusing boys which are sensitive to feminist problematising of social constructions of masculinity, and which are congruent with expectations for change both in terms of personal responsibility and social accountability for the development of sustainable, nonabusive discourses and articulations of masculine subject positioning.

We frame our expanded discussion of Gee's (1991) linguistic tools for narrative analysis in terms of a range of *'interpretive questions'* raised by each of his five hierarchically more inclusive analytic levels. Following Gee, we suggest that by helping to focus and anchor interpretive activity in specific, warrantable textual/ linguistic structures of sense-making, these questions *provide constraints on multiple possible meanings* so that 'many answers are ruled out by the structure of the text' (Gee, 1991: 16). This includes restraining professional interpretive appropriations by instead privileging a view of people's texts as purposeful and replete with 'inordinately rich meaning and structure' (Gee, 1992: 232), that is, positively discriminating in favour of participants' meanings and resources for meaning-making. In the context of *transcription including co-participants*, these questions, we argue, also serve a reflexive function in relation to analysis of how the researcher's questions organise and constrain the interviewee's responses, as well as highlighting how the interviewee's responses to these core questions are organised to raise their own structural pointers towards 'acceptable interpretations' (Gee, 1991: 15). We note that while the *recognition of a power-differential* between PE/the research interviewer and Lance as participant is important, at the same time Lance's contribution to the interpretation of PE's questions and responses is critically significant to how the thematic focus develops and, in this sense, there is *also a discursive parity* which can appropriately be heard as jointly exercised. We propose that the use of Gee's levels of analysis for *thematic interpretation is not linear, but recursive*, intended to achieve an overall, interactive warranting responsive to the range of interpretive questions, the principal aim of which is a demonstration of sense-making seen to emerge from the focused material across the levels of textual interpretation. We re-emphasise that a methodological objective was to maintain a balance between using the analytical tools for reading the text in terms of how it was *said*, and drawing on conceptual and theoretical material to interpret the co-construction of thematic meanings in relation, for instance, to dominant and/or counterhegemonic discourses.

Having reviewed Gee's *'micro' linguistic tools (pitch glide, idea units and lines)* we then introduce and demonstrate the *'macro' structural components of stanzas, strophes and parts*, with a view to defining the *methodological means and meaning of thematic interpretation*. We identify Q3 as our unit of narrative analysis, organising our discussion around three demonstrable parts into which it can be linguistically structured: Part 1 (discussed in Chapter 3) is focused on a gendered theme of stubbornness; Part 2 (discussed in Chapter 4) on a gendered theme of cleverness and Part 3 (discussed in Chapter 5) on a gendered theme of choosing school options. We show how, triggered by PE's formulations of Q3, each theme arises out of and is intimately connected with narratives of learning 'in terms of growing up as a boy in your family'. We argue that in the transition out of Q2, setting a context within which PE first asks Q3, Lance positions himself through a normative gendered account of loving to solve 'other people's problems' but hating to have 'to solve my own'. This account, we suggest, draws on discourses of 'problem solving' viewed as a major site for social practices of hegemonic masculinity that sustain power and control as well as promote the myth of autonomy at the expense of personal and interpersonal emotional connectedness and vulnerability (e.g. Seidler, 1994; Connell, 1995). As a context for Q3, specifically in relation to gender, the Q2 transition implicitly raises two questions – Does Lance or does he not want to solve the problem of his sexual abusing? and if he does, how can he learn to be as effective to solve his own problems as he feels he is at solving others? Both these questions are clearly relevant to therapeutic work.

Across our thematic interpretation of Q3, we argue that Lance's *narrative accounts* of his learning about being or becoming a boy in his family are *performative*: they simultaneously *involve active discursive positioning, reflexively* in relation to himself be(com)ing 'a boy', *and rhetorically* in terms of the interactional work of his telling in the context of the research interview. As the basis for analysis, we *provide our transcription* of Q3/Part 1 showing our application of Gee's micro- and macro-linguistic tools to this stretch of interview discourse. We introduce the idea of *'headlines'*, which we suggest *emerge through, as well as guide, a circular process of transcription/analysis* that begins with putting the analytical tools to use, results through closer listening and reading in new or adjusted understanding, and returns to the use of the analytical tools informed by developing interpretive responses. This approach, we suggest, reflects and helps to make transparent a trail of interpretive choices, which, in the presence of the text, can be reviewed and interrogated. This process of textual formatting, anchored in the invitations and the constraints of the text *as said*, is clearly able to integrate respondent and interviewer into the transcript, making available for analysis the co-creation both of questions and responses which constitute the linguistic flow of conversation. Precisely these points, we suggest, are typically overlooked in appropriative, de-contextualised and 'top down' approaches to textual interpretation.

We then introduce and illustrate our use of Gee's (1991) five interpretive levels of structure and meaning, conceived hierarchically and contributing to thematic analysis. We describe and offer examples of how *the ways in which a text is said can provide micro- and macro-cues raising interpretive questions that help to privilege speakers' sense-making.* Thus, these levels may be thought of, not as invariant linguistic structures such as Labov's clausal functions, but as *text-based areas of reflexive enquiry*, each raising particular interpretive questions, which was summarised in Table 3.1. These questions, furthermore, both *invite attention to wider social contexts and canonical narratives, and constrain the ways in which these can be used* or 'imported' as interpretive lenses for reading narrative texts. They serve to *rebalance power in favour of respondent meaning-making, by supporting the position that ideological or canonical material must be interpreted from and in light of emphasised or focused material evident from how the text was said.* This is particularly important, and notoriously easily ignored, in relation to interpretive readings of personal narratives, typically triggered by social 'breaches' and, therefore, typically subject(ed) to expert knowledges and interpretive frameworks, moral/political as well as clinical – such as those of sexually abusing boys. It is precisely for such reasons that we have emphasised how retheorising the field of our research interest is inseparably connected to our choice of methodology.

Anchoring our analysis in the available text, drawing illustratively on a range of tools and ideas, we systematically argue across Q3/Part 1 that Lance is actively practising to position himself in relation to his mother and father in particular gendered ways that he wants PE to understand. These include evaluations of his parents' relative and/or differential power in relation to home and to the world of work, as well as his own uncertain status still as a child and also as a boy, as he works to account for why at home 'it always seems' that 'what the women want we get'. What emerges, we suggest, is an explanatory and exemplary theme of 'stubbornness', identified with his mother, which Lance finds not only satisfactory for making narrative sense of the experience he is accounting for, but which, because he expresses admiration for it, creates some contradictions for him with social narratives of adult masculinity and the world of work (identified with his father). We argue, in particular, that Lance's *personal narrative* account of his gendered learning in his family discursively positions him through this telling as ambivalently if not actively engaged in *not* supporting a family or *cultural discourse* in which the status of his father's/men's work constitutes domestic status through absence. Instead, situating himself in a preferred relationship to his mother's 'stubbornness', Lance orients PE to view his emotional development or investments 'as a boy' in ways that reflect both his ambivalence about and perhaps *resistance to hegemonic gendered social narratives and assumptions* available for making sense of himself to himself, and for situating himself in relation to others.

Doing thematic interpretation

In Chapter 4, we continue to extend our example, using Part 2 of Q3, focusing on the practicalities and persistence needed for doing thematic interpretation based on the intimate and detailed work of close textual analysis. Situated theoretically as we have described, we demonstrate the use of micro- and macro-linguistic structures, building on cues to preferred sense-making which the various levels of interpretive questions suggest in the context of the interview as jointly constructed. We argue that to make the transition from simply *claiming* to effectively *practising* theoretical commitment to resist ascriptivism and to respectfully privilege 'the remarkable subtleness and sophistication of ordinary people's talk and its designed features' (Edley and Wetherell, 1997: 205), requires repetitive listening and persistent engagement at close quarters with the transcribed text. While we recognise that this kind of work can be daunting and at times confusing, we demonstrate that in the interplay between working interpretively at micro and macro levels of the text the *use of 'headlines' can help to organise and, in this sense, transparently account for the interpretive directions taken as the text unfolds*. We demonstrate the potential of critical narrative analysis to develop closely warranted, extended and sustained thematic interpretation of the interview as discourse, including the important capacity to generate links with wider canonical narratives and other interpretive frameworks, which do not constitute importation or appropriation of specious 'order' or 'coherence', but may be seen to flow from the focusing system and 'traces' in the text itself.

Since the principle point of this chapter is the demonstration itself, we will briefly summarise the main themes of our analysis to mark the development of our particular thematic interpretation, pointing to particular links we make between the content and performative activity of Lance's narrative accounts, and wider interpretive frameworks of hegemonic and counterhegemonic masculine identities. In Part 2 of Q3, we argue that Lance develops an account of his gendered learning in his family across a *series of personal narratives*: first, concerning his experience of his parents' views of schooling for their sons and daughters; second, concerning a canonical rumour about the relative 'cleverness' of men and women, about which he makes a clear evaluation offering a gratuitous link to 'the offending'; third, illustrating gendered cleverness through the story of building a rabbit run expressing ambivalent admiration for his mother's/women's 'cleverness'; fourth, further exploring this ambivalence in terms of how he used his mother's cleverness to improve his schoolwork. Across these narratives, we suggest, Lance is both *accounting for and practising to situate* himself in relation to dilemmas in his experience around possible and acceptable masculine identities. After distinguishing two gendered pathways through school, determined for his sisters by the view that to get what they want girls need to be 'pushed', and for himself that boys will only work if they 'want' to, Lance connects this family experience with an explanatory *canonical rumour* that 'men are supposed to be more clever' than women. Practising to situate himself at least in principle in relation to this rumour, which he assumes that PE as well has heard, Lance asserts a *counterhegemonic view*, that it is 'not actually true', in a way that inverts or subverts the male-as-norm by concluding men are 'just as clever as what women are'. While we recognise that naming this view and investment in it are not the same, we argue that in negotiating his own psychological perspective, Lance effectively *elevates a demoted view of women's 'cleverness' that contradicts or at least challenges the canonical rumour.*

This becomes a basis for, first, broadly characterising the gendered cleverness of women in terms of thinking things out, and then making a specific contrast with his own reputation for not thinking of 'the consequences of doing something...not particularly the offending, but...anything'. This contrast construes *'offending' not as deviant from but typical of his own male 'cleverness' in relation to 'anything'*, thus creating dilemmas around negotiating a sense of masculine identity in relation to his mother and father. Our analysis of Lance's narrative of building the rabbit run suggests that to the extent that he *discursively invests himself in a preference* for his mother's/women's kind of 'cleverness' he at the same time expresses an increasing *ambivalence functioning, in effect, as irresolution*. We suggest that this is not simply about whether what he says he always wanted to 'be', that is, like his mother/women in being 'able to plan things out', is or is not *really* what he wants to become, but may also reflect an *absence of, or uncertainty about, discourses for articulating and making this kind of cleverness available for masculine subject positioning*. We point out that while 'grooming' certainly involved Lance in planning ahead in the interests of abuse, this male appropriation is clearly not what he means or illustrates by his mother's kind of cleverness with 'good detail'. His ambivalence about how to admire her kind of cleverness, which others say he lacks and he says he wants, and at the same time to sustain an acceptable view of himself, includes such a *precarious mix of admiration and devaluation* that it leads to Lance's need to reclaim in PE's eyes what he admires in his mother by correcting a possible misapprehension he may have generated with the paradoxical disclaimer that 'I wouldn't say mum's stupid'.

Overall, across Part 2, we argue that there appear to be no normative or acceptable discourses available through which to practice views of himself and his wants that include both his identification with his father as masculine and identification with a kind of cleverness socially devalued for him as a boy by virtue of being connected to his mother/women. In suggesting that his admiration effectively situates him as a boy member of some subordinated masculinity, we do not suggest that this automatically constitutes a resistance to hegemonic masculinity, but rather that Lance's *ambivalence around this admiration may provide a context for meaning-making within which 'not offending' could make important and gendered sense*. In terms of utility, this possibility has bearing on accountability and social justice, in part because it invites approaches to therapy attuned to the possibilities of discursive reconstruction or 'reauthoring' (White and

Epston, 1990) around different narratives of masculine identities. Thus, in light of our theoretical orientation, we demonstrate across Q3/Part 1 the kind of close and extended textual work necessary to doing thematic interpretation in which, in the context of its co-construction, Lance's own 'meaning-sense' is privileged, wider social and interpretive discourses engaged with, and both are anchored in the 'trace in the talk'.

Moving analysis to a more molar level

In Chapter 5, completing our overall analysis of the Q3 interview text, we draw somewhat back from the intensive and extended micro-work with Part 2, and demonstrate using Part 3 a way in which narratives can be examined in terms of relationships between the more 'molar' components of the material, while at the same time warranting from within the discourse structures or cues of the text itself increased attention to the presence and effects of cultural discourses. We pursue a focus on demonstrating thematic coherence, foregrounding 'chunks' of text evident from the use of macro-linguistic transcription tools (stanzas, strophes and parts), along with selective micro-analysis, guided by the outline or 'trail' of interpretive headlines. The headlines generated through the work of transcription, which we present as an overall outline of this stretch of text (Table 5.1), suggest an organisational development analysable in terms of three strophic or thematically connected 'chunks' showing traceable stanzaic coherence. In the context of their co-construction, these chunks, we argue, can also be seen to be recursively interconnected in the sense that Lance is engaged in a subtle and complex process of discursive positioning and repositioning himself in relation to PE's recycling of the core Q3 and ways in which he follows this up. Our analysis suggests that Lance first situates himself from the perspective of his family experience in relation to an account of parental support for choice or self-determination in making his entry from the world of school into the world of work. This account is then elaborated in terms of a highly specific context of socially constructed gendered identities: school and the choices of 'Options'. Dilemmas and possibilities of hegemonic and counterhegemonic masculine identities are discursively accounted for and performed, in part through Lance's reflexive dramatisation of possible consequences of particular courses of decision-making. Finally, closure of this section of Part 3 is accomplished, by relocating the theme of 'choice making' in the context of the family discourse of self-determination, as well as overall closure of Q3.

We review our analytic movement across Part 3 with particular attention to links with wider social discourses and possible signs of alternative counterhegemonic subject positions and practices. After expressing appreciation of how his parents encouraged both himself and his sisters to 'make your own decisions', Lance then gives an account of practising to situate himself in relation to highly stereotyped gendered subject positions defined by 'choice making' amongst school Options, which may be understood from *within the text* in terms of 'studying masculinity as a discursive practice' (Wetherell and Edley, 1998: 165). In contrasting Lance's Part 2 and Part 3 narratives of family gender differences in relation to school, we suggest that *variability* of accounts represents not contradiction or inconsistency of some 'essential' story, but suggests contextual differences in relation to the discursive performance of *different interactional work at different points during the interview*. We argue that stating the obvious or the unremarkable, that is, about the gender stereotyping of Options, is not trivial; but that by doing so *Lance positions himself reflexively*, as a kind of participant observer rather than submerged within the orbit of the discursive and social practices that made up this school experience. We argue that to *the extent that the stereotypes are interpreted as unremarkable, their power is unquestioned/constitutive in its prevention of alternative choices of gendered identities*. However, Lance's articulation of these stereotypes enables him to highlight his own active participation in considering possibilities and consequences of his own masculine subject positioning in relation to discourses and social/school practices that, as givens, he neither rejects nor accepts. Rather, in recounting his thinking about the consequences of choosing girls' Options, he is aware that the available categories of how 'school is different...for boys and girls' would constitute, in terms of gendered identity, a difference leaving him both alone among the girls and apart from the boys.

We do not suggest that it is possible from this text to determine whether or to what extent Lance's account of this thinking represents counterhegemonic discourse practices. However, what we do suggest is the *fundamental importance of narrative itself as a discursive practice* employed by Lance through and by means of which he can be 'heard' to be actively engaged in making sense of himself as a boy in relation to dominant discourses and social practices constitutive of available institutionalised subject positions of girls and of other boys. At the same time, however, we argue that in part Lance is accomplishing interactional work to the extent that through his accounts he is clearly situating himself in relation to PE and to Q3 as *thinking on the margins of the dominant discourses* he reflects on. For instance, neither his accounts of his preferences for his mother's 'stubbornness' and 'cleverness', nor those of his decision for a girls' option, are extended or obtain 'the *authorisation* of the hegemonic masculinity of the dominant group' (Connell, 1995: 81); but, at least to *that* extent, they *may be appropriately interpreted as discursive means by which marginalised subject positions are interrogated and/or interrogate certain dominant discourses and discourse practices of masculine identity*. The degree to which Lance's narratives express ambivalence around these subject positionings does not discredit how he accounts for or practices them, but rather, we argue, may serve to *hold open and unresolved his culturally normative 'moment of engagement' with hegemonic masculinity* (Connell, 1995). This ambivalence may also potentially *provide resources for the development of therapeutic conversations* around alternative subject positions of masculine identity in which he already shows some investment and skill and which could, perhaps, constitute an empowering basis for learning how to 'love' to become effective to solve the problems of his offending.

The therapeutic nurturing of such counterhegemonic narratives and congruent social practices is more likely to be attractive to treatment approaches that themselves constitute 'counterhegemonic' responses to dominant social discourses (e.g. McNamee and Gergen, 1992; Franklin, 1995) than to those invested in consolidating prevailing theoretical or 'scientific' formulations of sexually abusing boys. In this wider social context, it is clearly important to recognise that the social construction of a 'gender project' configured by language, social practices, discourses and available subject positions generating and sustaining individuals' responsibilities for sexual violence, and aiming 'to establish respectful and sensitive relationships' (Jenkins, 1990: 32), may itself risk subjugation in the field of contested masculinities. However, rather than marginalising, for example, Lance's personal narrative accounts through subordination or appropriation to dominant institutional formulations, critical narrative analysis helps to draw attention to possible resources for change already available, as well as possible directions for preferred future change. While this approach strongly focuses and enhances personal responsibility for change, it also serves to situate personal narrative sense-making so that social accountabilities are foregrounded and may continue to be problematised and challenged. In particular, critical narrative analysis, privileging the narrator's own words and points of view, offers a discursively warrantable psychosocial awareness of how 'culture "speaks itself" through an individual's story' (Riessman, 1993: 5). Moreover, it provides an index of emerging personal narrative material in which contradictions, uncertainties and ambivalences may be understood in terms of irresolutions around engagement with dominant discourses and social practices reflecting an absence of available alternative replacement discourses with which to re-story and construct alternative identities.

The work described in these analytic chapters is clearly painstaking, demanding of the researcher considerable patience and an interest in detail. In addition, it can seem impossibly daunting when one is faced with analysing relatively sizeable amounts of data – in this connection, implying more than a very small number of participants. By contrast, qualitative approaches such as grounded theory (Charmaz, 2003) or discourse analysis (Willig, 2003), hardly known for their huge sample sizes, are apparently more efficient or at least economical. However, there are numerous attributes of critical narrative analysis that are not only theoretically compelling, but also amenable to practical implementation across a range of studies. First, the theoretical congruence of this approach with social constructionist and deconstructionist endeavours has already been noted, and is shared with other forms of discursive analysis. However, critical narrative analysis adds to this the further theoretical and ethical edge of valuing individual lives; that is, in common with some case study approaches derived from therapeutic traditions, each individual speaker's narrative is studied in detail for its own sake, for what it says of that person's subjectivity and subject positioning, rather than as something necessarily exemplary or generalisable. The specificity of personal accounting is thus stressed and validated, while at the same time placed in a context of social positioning.

On the practical side, the demands of the approach can be validated and ameliorated, depending on the research context. We have tried to demonstrate how the rigorous 'ground up' approach, from pitch glide to general 'Part' and theme, can result in a compelling portrait of the 'on-line' constructive processes of self-narrativising engaged in by an active speaker in interaction with a questioning other. This represents a comprehensive use of the approach, in which each level of analysis is conscientiously and reciprocally grounded in the details of the 'lower' level, so generating careful and reflexive 'bottom up' interpretation. However, it is also possible to use the narrative analytic approach more strategically, to thicken out or root more global thematic work. Researchers might, for example, do conventional thematic analytic investigations identifying content-based themes across an interview or series of interviews, but then employ narrative analytic procedures to investigate particular passages of text in detail. Such passages would be selected on theoretical or methodological grounds: for example, sections of text marked by intense emotionality, contradictions or conflicts, particularly fragmentary narratives or especially rounded stories, obvious 'breaches' or possibly simply unique statements or claims. Indeed, it can be argued that this is what we have done in this book: selected out especially informative parts of Lance's interview text and subjected them to detailed critical scrutiny. The sheer mass of narrative data with which one is often faced commonly makes such an approach, based on a principled and open selectivity, a necessity.

Counterclaims and contestations

This section is intended to review but not necessarily resolve a number of counterclaims and contestations affecting our positioning and practice of critical narrative analysis. For convenience we will organise these under various headings, although inevitably they overlap and mutually inform one another. Two broad fronts inviting objection and continuing debate, that is, feminist and social constructionist thinking and practice, which we have drawn on to make overt our own theory base and to demonstrate the inseparability of theory and method, are beyond the limits this section aims to review. Instead, our focus is on concerns and possible objections specifically arising from our approach as applied, developed and demonstrated in practice.

Validation and generalisability

It has not been our aim to 'prove' the methodologies that we have employed, but to broadly situate and then specifically apply the 'turn to text' in relation to feminist and social constructionist theory. Nevertheless, some discussion of validity is appropriate since one fundamental and likely area of objection is to what extent our various claims (e.g. from those that are theoretically and politically thematic, to those concerning micro-interpretations within particular bits of texts) have any validity and generalisability or utility, particularly given that we have considered only one interview text in this book. It has, of course, been a significant aim of this book to make a case for analytical and interpretive claims derived from theorised and linguistically anchored close readings of texts, in particular, as Edley and Wetherell (1997: 205) put it, 'highlighting the remarkable subtleness and sophistication of ordinary people's talk and its *designed* features'. However, reservations around validity and generalisability are important, not least because methodological invalidation could suggest 'political' invalidation, sustaining the further criticism that discourse and narrative analytic work stops short at 'discourse discourse' and serves no 'progressive use' (Parker, 1992: 93).

Mishler (1990: 417–23) has addressed the issue of *validation* specifically in relation to narrative studies. He starts 'by reformulating validation as the social construction of knowledge', suggesting that 'trustworthiness rather than truth displaces validation from its traditional location' and is developed on the basis of what he designates as 'candidate exemplars' or specific models of exemplary research practice. That this approach has become central to the development of narrative studies is broadly illustrated by the range and diversity of 'exemplars' found in Riessman (2008) and Andrews *et al.* (2008). Mishler's (1990) aim is not to reject, for example, traditional scientific criteria such as 'reliability, falsifiability, and objectivity', but rather to challenge their hegemony, arguing that they 'must be understood as particular ways of warranting validity claims rather than as universal, abstract guarantors of truth'. This understanding of validation 'makes issues of meaning and interpretation central', focusing attention on ways in which the social world is 'constructed in and through our discourse and actions'. Clearly both discourse and narrative analysis as qualitative and interpretive research methodologies share in the theoretical assumptions informing Mishler's perspective on validation, and may contribute to the reflexive processes of evaluating the 'trustworthiness' of particular 'observations, interpretations, and generalisations' (p. 419). Mishler notes three commonalities from his range of 'candidate exemplars' which, he suggests, are critical for the validation of narrative studies: (1) 'the display of the primary texts'; (2) 'specification of analytic categories... in terms of discernible features of the texts'; (3) 'theoretical interpretations focused on structures' (p. 437). We will briefly comment below on each of these in relation to our approach.

(1) Throughout, we have strongly emphasised the importance both of displaying primary texts and of recognising how interpretation is affected by differing ways of displaying or transcribing texts. Displaying primary texts enables others to inspect and assess the methods used and interpretations offered, as well as to make at least some preliminary judgements of how representative a given text may be of other texts and, to this extent, to consider the inferred or projected *generalisability* of research claims on the basis of an evaluation of trustworthiness or plausibility rather than in terms of 'proof' or 'truth'. Displaying their interview texts also provides a basis for the absent narrators/participants themselves to retain some control over their own words, which must at least be appealed to, ideally in the contexts of their co-construction, as a basis for interpretation. (2) We have gradually introduced a range of specific analytic categories both illustrated from and used to enter into the given primary texts. These ranged from macro-linguistic categories such as stanzas, strophes and parts, to micro-categories such as pitch glide, idea units and lines. (3) In the work of textual analysis, the various analytic categories were employed to interpret patterns or structures of relationship at different levels discernible in and through the primary texts. In particular, critical narrative analysis allows the constitutive patterning of 'talk and text' to be linked to the power of dominant social discourses that can be seen both to provide discursive resources for their own reproduction and to restrain or prevent alternative articulations and associated subject positionings. At the same time, amongst other aspects of narrative sense-making, this approach can be used to

identify patterns of textual evidence highlighting discernible reflexive and evaluative discourses and discourse practices (or 'experi-
ments') as at least potential resources for individuals' therapeutic
change and as signs or indicators contesting social norms.

We have also noted (in Chapter 1) a significant further development related to the conceptualisation of 'exemplars' and the theme
of validity: it is the concern that narrative continuity or 'coherence'
has been too culturally central in the process of 'demonstrating trustworthiness' (Riessman and Quinney, 2005: 188–9). Instead, it is
being argued that greater theoretical, including linguistic, and analytical attention needs to be paid to sense-making of 'fractured
accounts' (Mishler, 2006: 45) and 'disrupted narratives' (Riessman,
2008: 190), for example, in 'stories of trauma survivors' (ibid.: 191),
and to what Frosh (2007) proposes as 'maintaining the vision of a
subject in fragments', which includes engaging with contingency in
the domain of 'validity' such that researchers' production of knowledge is reflexively 'construed as the closure of theory around an arbi-
trary fixed point' (Frosh and Baraitser, 2008: 13). We demonstrate our
own concern with this through attention to contradictions, uncertainties and irresolutions evident at some points across the 'Lance'
texts, and in our commitment to resist 'foreclosure' typically driven,
for instance, by cultural and professional expectations of in effect
appropriative, 'top down' 'coherence'.

Thus, the question of validation and the related question of *generalisability* may be addressed, not in terms of claims for 'abstract' or
unitary findings more typical of traditional research goals and dominant formulations, but rather in terms recommending an approach
to research as sense-making, rooted in commitment to participants'
orientations because their discourse practices have 'genuine consequences for people's lives' (Potter and Wetherell, 1987: 170). We have
invited critical scrutiny of such 'validation' in relation to our own
research both in terms of working to be transparent about 'the situated perspective and traditions that frame it' (Riessman, 2008: 185),
and through fine-grained 'bottom up' interpretations 'grounded in a
close study of the particular' (ibid.: 18). From this perspective, our
aim has been to warrant interpretations of particular texts which,
while not claiming to be *the* only reading, may stand alongside other
possible interpretations (including for instance those constructed on
the basis of 'scientific method') as sufficiently warranted to consider

plausible or 'trustworthy' and hence able to contribute to changes in thinking and practice.

Polarising and plausibility

We have argued that the paradigm shift, as Stivers (1993) summarises it, from *the* framework to *a* framework in the social sciences is not dismissive of the claims of positivist science but rather both supports an inclusive attitude to methodologies and expects greater professional transparency regarding theoretical and value assumptions. Goldstein (1997) characterises this shift in terms of the question of 'plausibility'. This involves highlighting professional responsibility for choices (theoretical and methodological) which are not value-neutral but rather privilege differing perspectives with differing 'prescriptive' implications which, in turn, serve to warrant plausibility in terms of particular assumptions and effects (a process, that is, typifying Mishler's (1990) reflexive understanding of validation as social construction). In our worked example of interviews with a sexually abusing boy, this involves a set of questions around whether or to what extent the theoretical and methodological commitment not to efface or appropriate the boy's own words and sense-making elicits different understandings of how he makes sense of his sexual abusing and what different implications this may suggest for 'consolidating' or challenging dominant therapeutic approaches. Indirectly, it also calls social accountability into question, in terms of the extent to which dominant discourses, constituting and enforced by abusive masculine identities and social practices, may also organise or restrain prevailing systems of social justice contextualising dominant assessment and treatment 'packages'.

We are thus arguing that the employment of critical narrative analysis does not constitute a polarisation of research approaches, but rather a choice within an inclusive range of possible investigative strategies. Mishler's (1996: 90–1) suggestion, made in relation to case-based narrative analysis, that '(w)e may have already passed the point where we have to begin... analysis by contrasting it with the dominant paradigm', both indicates an increasing acceptance of research practices theorised and operationalised in social constructionist terms of plurality and plausibility, and strongly invites the combination and inclusive 'diversity of narrative models' by means of any and all of which, in different ways, 'we construct the story and its meaning' (Mishler, 1995: 117). This may, for example, involve the elaboration of diverse 'exemplars' using a range of specifically narrative analytic strategies (e.g. Andrews *et al.*, 2008), constructing a multi-levelled narrative 'orientation' (Hiles and Čermák, 2008), utilising narrative analysis in relation to psychoanalytic theory (Frosh and Baraitser, 2008; Frosh and Young, 2008), or integrating narrative analysis with other 'forms of investigation' (Wetherell, 2008: 80).

Relativism, reflexivity and responsibility

It may be objected that in privileging the voices or sense-making of research participants, some of the 'critical' element of critical narrative analysis is lost. This is particularly the case when, as in our example, the participants are representative of groups held to have engaged in dubious, deceitful or destructive activities and who could be suspected of using the research situation to exculpate themselves. The implied charge is that an inevitable collusion occurs in which personal responsibility (here, for abusing) gets lost or watered down by the relativism of multiple interpretations. This objection is especially significant because of the degree of moral revulsion, moral panic, social disapprobation and high-profile/high-expense treatment responses to the 'discovery' of younger and younger sexually abusing boys, and the prevailing professional view that 'offender self reports are usually unreliable' (Hoghughi *et al.*, 1997: 56). Our argument, however, is that critical narrative analysis allows a researcher to privilege participants' accounts and meaning-making, in their own words and from their own points of view, while at the same time interrogating those accounts, restraining foreclosure both in terms of constitutive dominant discourses as well as the personal narrative material arising through interviews. This balance can be addressed in two main ways: one in relation to concerns about relativism, the other in relation to a number of issues around textual interpretation.

Bruner (1990: 27) argues that the so-called 'problem of relativism' does not lead necessarily to an 'anything goes' position, but, on the contrary, may serve to make overt the importance of 'an unpacking of presuppositions, the better to explore one's commitments'. This cuts two ways, with effects on professionals and on approaches to research and therapeutic work with clients. Bruner suggests the significance of reflexivity in helping to make us 'aware of our own perspective and those of others when we make our claims of "rightness" and "wrongness" ' (p. 25). This view is congruent with Goldstein's (1997) emphasis, discussed above, on the increased accountability (and exposure) of professionals for their (often unstated and unmarked) choices of model or metaphor amongst a plurality of possible perspectives each with differing prescriptive effects and implications, for example, for research and therapy. It also fits with Gergen's (1994: 160) argument that social constructionism views the individual 'as self-reflexive and thus capable of autonomous change', thereby restoring 'the concept of personal responsibility to the repertoire of evaluative terms' (p. 172). From this perspective, for example, we have argued that the privileging of an individual boy's personal narrative sense-making serves to enhance attention to personal responsibility both for abusing and for changing in terms of accountability for agency and subject positioning. That is, it promulgates a view of the 'choosing subject' actively engaged in discursively positioning himself in relation to available dominant discourses. Thus, instead of losing or compromising personal responsibility, attention to the discursive instability and plurality of socially constructed masculine subject positions serves both to strongly focus personal responsibility in terms of personal choice and accountability for abusive and for changed subject positioning, as well as to problematise social accountability in relation to collusive dominant discourses.

Interpretation and transcription

Following Mishler (1986, 1994), we have been critical of decontextualised transcription, both in the sense of extracting 'bits' of text from the context and process in which their emergence is embedded, and, in particular, the typical elision of the researcher from the joint construction of interview texts. However, emphasising the diversity and plurality of interpretive possibilities directly related to differing displays of primary texts, may raise again in a somewhat different form the problem and potential objection of relativism. What, after all, is *the text*? If every 'display' results in different interpretations, does the plurality of possible meanings invalidate any particular interpretation?

Initially defining and discussing specific narrative analytic categories in terms of discernible features of primary texts, we illustrated how differing displays of text or representations of discourse bring forth different meanings. In part the aim was to demonstrate Mishler's (1991: 255) assertion that transcription is not simply a 'neutral' 'technical' exercise, but is theory driven and serves rhetorical ends, reflecting assumptions articulated through 'interpretive practice', and that, therefore, as Riessman (1993: 60) points out, 'analysis cannot be easily distinguished from transcription', in part because the process of transcription is 'inseparable from language theory' (Riessman, 2008: 29) Recognising this also makes evident that linguistic tools for discourse and narrative analysis are neither neutral in themselves nor employed neutrally. Thus, drawing attention to how differing displays of texts, differing conventions of transcription, support differing theoretical commitments, highlights the importance of researcher transparency about, or accountability for, assumptions and responsibility for choice in light of intentions and implications.

Our own theoretical assumptions, drawing on feminist and social constructionist thinking and practice, generate a methodological preference for forms of transcription privileging the words of interviewees and at the same time reflecting the interview as discourse, that is, enabling analysis of the joint-production or social construction of personal narrative material. In contrast to this, many discourse practices of 'institutional narratives', rooted in large part in information 'gleaned' from clients themselves, nevertheless can tend to appropriate personal meaning-making through professional acts of interpretation informed by powerful asymmetries of expertise anchored in 'invisible' yet constitutive assumptions, values and norms, effectively resulting in 'using the clients' own stories against them' (Holmes, 1997: 155). These acts of interpretation, at the level of transcription, on the one hand, often involve the inclusion of de-contextualised 'snippets' of client discourse, leaving them vulnerable to impositions of expert meaning-making, while, on the other, they selectively marginalise variations in accounts that do not fit with dominant and desired categories. By contrast, the theoretical rationale founding critical narrative analysis for privileging interviewees' personal narrative material is congruent with a methodological approach to the display of text including researcher and participant contributions which, in turn, involve implications for more reflexive and open kinds of analytic work and understandings of narrative material. While no display represents 'objective reality', the analytical work permitted by the dialogic display of the interview as discourse draws attention, for instance, to the contextualised co-creation of the personal narrative material both in terms of 'content' and of its interactional work.

Limits of interpretation: ranging from acceptable to impossible

Even if the dangers of relativism are allayed in relation to an interpretive plurality of differing displays of text, this does not solve the problem of multiple possible interpretations of 'the same' text and how, or whether, one or any of these may be viewed as trustworthy. This objection concerns the question of the limits of interpretation: if not 'anything' goes, then how are acceptable or plausible interpretations distinguished from impossible or implausible ones?

Gee (1991: 37) proposes a broad distinction between 'two different uses of discursive language': one, reportative, from which when successful 'the hearer can reconstruct the model'; the other, inviting thematic interpretation, enabling the hearer to 'reconstruct a certain part of a philosophy of life from a particular point of view'. This distinction contributes to an understanding of how, for example, institutional narratives (e.g. assessment processes and reports) may appropriate or efface a narrator's own words and points of view in the interests of a 'model' or powerful 'master' narrative and dominant discourses. In contrast, commitment to 'ways of working with texts so that the original narrator is not effaced' (Riessman, 1993: 34) involves learning to become, Gee (1999: 109) suggests, 'an appropriate hearer', that is, one paying attention to the structures and contextualisation cues of a narrator's text which indicate 'their *viewpoint* on the information and the interaction' (p. 106). Gee's (e.g. 1991) theory and conventions for narrative analysis provide means for entering into texts which privilege a narrator's meaning-making within definable and discernible limitations of interpretation. We have outlined and employed Gee's methodology involving five analytical levels and related interpretive questions, the fifth and most comprehensive, that is 'thematic interpretation', being anchored in the 'focusing system' of the other four. This methodology enables analysis of interview material to include a significant degree of reflexivity around any interpretive claims. In our worked example, this occurs by interrogating and thus warranting *what* the researcher learned from a boy, about *'How you see things'*, from the point of view of the further question *'How did I learn this?'* Gee's analytical categories, however, are not intended to be used to 'prove' one 'true' interpretation of a text, but in the interests of reconstructing a 'certain part of a philosophy of life from a particular point of view'. In the context of recognising that there are always many possible readings or hearings, their use helps both restrain 'many impossible readings' and at the same time 'constrain what counts as senseful (appropriate, fair) reading' (ibid.: 33). This linguistic approach, particularly when expanded to include the interview as discourse, is capable of warranting, for instance, thematic interpretation and cues to heterogeneities and contesting perspectives, including patterns of 'irresolution', while at the same time overtly including detailed analysis of how, inevitably, the interviewer 'as listener/interpreter is part of the text' (Riessman, 1993: 18). It also displays, once again, the relationship between a researcher's assumptions and the 'trace in the text', an issue of particular significance when (as in our worked example) choices of theoretical orientation involve a critical standpoint in relation to 'the researched' and to their particular texts. The ethical and political challenge to engage in interpretive work so the narrator is not effaced continues to be central in terms of the 'search for ways to return authority to narrators' (Andrews *et al.*, 2008: 154) in the multiple and complex psychosocial contexts to which the diversity of narrative studies addresses itself.

Interpretation: overinterpretation and intentionality

A further related, and concluding, area of potential objection to our approach, concerns the extent to which the activities of 'interpretation', even within the kinds of limits suggested above and in terms of 'bottom up' practices, may simply be a reading-into, an imputation or investment of meanings in texts not necessarily intended by their narrators. This further concern around interpretation can be fruitfully considered in terms of a positive discrimination in favour of meaning which, at times, may lead to taking a calculated risk of overinterpretation and suggest viewing intentionality from the perspective of the constraints and possibilities present in discourses available for the social construction of personal narrative meaning-making.

Believing that 'people's texts are not trivial outcomes of communicative needs' but are purposeful and replete with 'inordinately rich meaning and structure', Gee *et al.* (1992: 232–3) declare, as both a methodological statement and an ideological (e.g. anti-discriminatory) standpoint, that, in contrast to 'analyses that misconstrue the discourse of any person as meaningless or impoverished', they prefer to positively discriminate in favour of meaning and if necessary take the risk 'to err on the side of overinterpretation'. For example, in the analysis of L2/Q3 in Chapter 5, in support of a thematic interpretation suggesting that Lance's narrative material demonstrates active and 'experimental' subject positioning, we risk an 'over-interpretation' of Lance's articulation of himself as 'the ONLY BOY' considering a choice for a girls' Option, by arguing, in the context of impinging dominant discourses and sites of social practice constitutive of forms of hegemonic masculine identity, that Lance is 'THINKING' *on the margins* of the dominant discourses he reflects on. The aim of taking this risk is to highlight the possibility that a certain narrative ambivalence around Lance's preferred subject positioning may indicate not so much a lack of investment as an absence of available discourses sustaining articulations of 'alternative' masculine identities. In this case, the risk of overinterpretation is not in whether or not the particular theme of gendered ambivalence may be warranted both as Lance's 'concern within the interaction' and from its 'trace' in the text, but rather that thinking on the margins might be mistaken as a reading of determined 'counter-hegemonic' marginalisation and practice. This kind of interpretive risk-taking, therefore, grounded in textual warranting around both the 'story' and the rhetorically intentional work or performance of its telling, positively discriminates in favour of meaning-making from the perspective(s) of the text itself. Consequently, what constitutes the 'overinterpretation' may extend, but its rejection would not disqualify, some 'appropriate' and plausible hearing.

A major concern and perhaps liability of this approach is in the amount of warranting or anchoring in the text that is required both to leave adequate reflexive evidence of how one has tried *not* to appropriate the voice of the participant and at the same time to show how one has entered interpretively into the text, including reflexively around the co-production of the interview and its retrospective sense-making. Trying to do this sort of analytical work, particularly on an extended stretch of text, is a *tour de force* that inevitably falls somewhere between the 'snippets' (de-contextualised) approach we have been critical of and the kind of move Wetherell and Edley (1998: 163) propose towards work with 'extended bodies of data, involving larger samples of interaction, such that it becomes possible to identify discursive patterns or regularities across a wide variety of social and institutional contexts'. Mishler (1996: 89) suggests a similar kind of move in his comparative work on temporally ordered narratives looking for 'case-based' patterns of choice across 'longitudinal' trajectories in contrast to 'cross-sectional approaches'. Our argument is that the intense and painstaking interpretive work of critical narrative analysis is necessary if one wishes to demonstrate not so much a prefabricated coherence of a given individual's overdetermining 'intention' across an interview, but a collaborative discursive interaction through which the interviewee's own determined as well as on-line responses, interactively privileged by the interviewer, contribute to the overall shape of the interview, as at the same time do the limiting, constitutive constraints of particular chosen or presently available discourses, narrative resources and perspectives.

Conclusion

We have offered above, (a) a chapter-by-chapter summary and overview of the substantive claims made in this book and, (b) a review of some counterclaims or areas of potential objection with particular reference to theoretical and methodological issues. Our central and fundamental substantive claim is that research employing critical narrative analysis, committed to privileging rather than marginalising subjective and personal narrative meaning-making, can help to interrogate personal and dominant social discourses. Furthermore, critical narrative analysis can be used to validate personal meaning-making resources, perhaps in particular the active agentic 'capacity for reflexive conceptualisation' (Gergen, 1994: 157), by means of which alternative 'replacement discourses' and narratives may be created with the hope to 'promote a difference in the way people experience and act in their situations' (Saleebey, 1994: 357). Critical narrative analysis is thus not only a methodology allowing careful, grounded exploration of the traces of meaning as they appear in personal texts; it is also an actively questioning approach seeking possibilities for change.

References

Andrews, M., Squire, C. and Tamboukou, M. (eds) (2008) *Doing Narrative Research* Thousand Oaks, London: Sage Publications.

Araji, S.K. (1997) *Sexually Aggressive Children: Coming to Understand Them* Thousand Oaks, London: Sage Publications.

Baraitser, L. (2008) On Giving and Taking Offence. *Psychoanalysis, Culture and Society*, forthcoming.

Brody, H. (1998) Foreword. In T. Greenhalgh and B. Hurwitz (eds) *Narrative Based Medicine* London: BMJ Books.

Bruner, J. (1987) Life as Narrative. *Social Research* 54: 11–32.

Bruner, J. (1990) *Acts of Meaning* Cambridge, MA and London: Harvard University Press.

Burck, C. (2007) Book Reviews – Emerson and Frosh, Critical Narrative Analysis. *Journal of Family Therapy* 29: 289–91.

Burman, E. (1992) Developmental Psychology and Postmodern Child. In J. Doherty, E. Graham and M. Malek (eds) *Postmodernism and the Social Sciences* London: Macmillan.

Burman, E. (1994) *Deconstructing Developmental Psychology* London and New York: Routledge.

Burman, E. (2008) Commentary on Frosh and Baraitser's Psychoanalysis and Psychosocial Studies. *Psychoanalysis, Culture and Society*, forthcoming.

Byrne, N.O. and McCarthy, I.C. (1995) Abuse, Risk and Protection: A Fifth Province Approach to an Adolescent Sexual Offence. In C. Burke and B. Speed (eds) *Gender, Power and Relationships* London and New York: Routledge.

Cecchin, G. (1987) Hypothesising, Circularity and Neutrality: An Invitation to Curiosity. *Family Process* 26: 405–13.

Charmaz, K. (2003) Grounded Theory. In J. Smith (ed.) *Qualitative Psychology* London: Sage Publications.

Connell, R.W. (1987) *Gender and Power: Society, the Person and Sexual Politics* Oxford: Polity Press.

Connell, R.W. (1995) *Masculinities* Cambridge: Polity Press.

Edley, N. and Wetherell, M. (1997) Jockeying for position: The Construction of Masculine Identities. *Discourse and Society* 8(2): 203–17.

Edwards, D. and Potter, J. (1992) *Discursive Psychology* London: Sage Publications.

Elms, R. (1990) Hostility, Apathy, Silence and Denial: Inviting Abusive Adolescents to Argue for Change. In M. Durrant and C. White (eds) *Ideas for Therapy with Sexual Abuse* Adelaide, South Australia: Dulwich Centre Publications.

Emerson, P.D. (2000) *Narrative Analysis and Abusive Masculinity: An Approach to Researching Boys who Sexually Abuse Other Children* Unpublished PhD for Birkbeck College, University of London.

Emerson, P.D. and Frosh, S. (2001) Young Masculinities and Sexual Abuse: Research Contestations. *International Journal of Critical Psychology* 3: 72–93.

Erooga, M. and Masson, H. (2006) Children and Young People with Sexually Harmful or Abusive Behaviours: Underpinning Knowledge, Principles, Approaches and Service Provision. In M. Erooga and H. Masson (eds) *Children and Young People Who Sexually Abuse Others – Current Developments and Practice Responses* (2nd edn) London and New York: Routledge.

Fausel, D.F. (1998) Collaborative Conversations for Change: A Solution focused Approach to Family Centered Practice. *Family Preservation Journal* 3: 59–74.

Ford, H. (2006) *Women Who Sexually Abuse Children* Chichester: Wiley.

Foucault, M. (1977) *Discipline and Punish: The Birth of the Prison* London: Penguin.

Foucault, M. (1980) *Power/Knowledge: Selected Interviews and Other Writings 1972–1977*. Colin Gordon (ed.) New York and London: Harvester Wheatsheaf.

Franklin, C. (1995) Expanding the Vision of the Social Constructionist Debates: Creating Relevance for Practitioners. *Families in Society: The Journal of Contemporary Human Services* September 1995: 395–406.

Frosh, S. (2007) Disintegrating Qualitative Research. *Theory and Psychology* 17: 635–53.

Frosh, S. and Baraitser, L. (2008) Psychoanalysis and Psychosocial Studies. *Psychoanalysis, Culture and Society*, forthcoming.

Frosh, S. and Emerson, P.D. (2005) Interpretation and Over-Interpretation: Disputing the Meaning of Texts. *Qualitative Research* 5: 307–24.

Frosh, S. and Young, L.S. (2008) Psychoanalytic Approaches to Qualitative Psychology. In C. Willig and W. Stainton-Rogers (eds) *The Handbook of Qualitative Methods in Psychology* London: Sage.

Gee, J.P. (1991) A Linguistic Approach to Narrative. *Journal of Narrative and Life History* 1(1): 15–39.

Gee, J.P. (1992) *The Social Mind: Language, Ideology, and Social Practice* New York and London: Bergin and Garvey.

Gee, J.P. (1999) *An Introduction to Discourse Analysis: Theory and Method* London and New York: Routledge.

Gee, J.P., Michaels, S. and O'Connors, M.C. (1992) Discourse Analysis. In M.D. Le Compte, W.L. Millroy and J. Preistle (eds) *The Handbook of Qualitative Research in Education* London: Academic Press Inc.

Geertz, C. (1997) Learning with Bruner. *The New York Review of Books* Vol. XLIV(6): 22–4.

Gergen, K.J. (1994) *Toward Transformation in Social Knowledge* London: Sage.

Gergen, M.M. and Gergen, K.J. (1993) Narratives of the Gendered Body in Popular Autobiography. In R. Josselson and A. Lieblich (eds) *The Narrative Study of Lives, Volume 1* Newbury Park, CA and London: Sage.

Gilligan, C. (1982) *In a Different Voice: Psychological Theory and Women's Development* Cambridge, MA and London: Harvard University Press.

Glaser, D. and Frosh, S. (1993) *Child Sexual Abuse* London: Macmillan.

Goldstein, H. (1997) Victors or Victims? In D. Saleebey (ed.) *The Strengths Perspective in Social Work Practice* New York: Longman.

Gunnarson, B-L., Linell, P. and Nordberg, B. (eds) (1997) *The Construction of Professional Discourse* UK: Longman.

Haraway, D. (1988) Situated Knowledges: The Science Question in Feminism and the Privilege of Partial Perspective. *Feminist Studies* 14(3): 575–99.

Harre, R. and Moghaddam, F. (eds) (2003) *The Self and Others: Positioning Individuals and Groups in Personal, Political, and Cultural Contexts* Westport, CT and London: Praeger.

Henriques, J., Hollway, W., Urwin, C., Venn, C. and Walkerdine, V. (1998) *Changing the Subject* (2nd edn) London: Routledge.

Henry, S. and Milovanovic, D. (1996) *Constitutive Criminology* London: Sage

Henwood, K., Griffin, C. and Phoenix, A. (eds) (1998) *Standpoints and Differences: Essays in the Practice of Feminist Psychology* London: Sage.

Henwood, K.L. and Pidgeon, N.F. (1992) Qualitative Research and Psychological Theorising. *British Journal of Psychology* 83: 97–111.

Hiles, D.R. and Čermák, I. (2008) Narrative Psychology. In C. Willig and W. Stainton-Rogers (eds) *The Handbook of Qualitative Methods in Psychology* London: Sage.

Hoggett, P. (2008) What's the Hyphen? Reconstructing Psycho-Social Studies. *Psychoanalysis, Culture and Society*, forthcoming.

Hoghughi, M.S., Bhate, S.R. and Graham, F. (eds) (1997) *Working with Sexually Abusive Adolescents* London: Sage Publications.

Holmes, G.E. (1997) The Strengths Perspective and the Politics of Clienthood. In D. Saleebey (ed.) *The Strengths Perspective in Social Work Practice* New York: Longman.

Hollway, W. (1989) *Subjectivity and Method in Psychology* London: Sage.

Hook, D. (2008) Articulations between Psychoanalysis and Psychosocial Studies: Limitations and Possibilities. *Psychoanalysis, Culture and Society*, forthcoming.

Hyden, L-C. (1997) The Institutional Narrative as Drama. In B-L. Gunnarson *et al. The Construction of Professional Discourse* UK: Longman.

Jenkins, A. (1990) *Invitations to Responsibility* Adelaide: Dulwich Centre Publications.

Jefferson, T. (2008) What is 'the Psychosocial': A Response to Frosh and Baraitser. *Psychoanalysis, Culture and Society*, forthcoming.

Johnson, T.C. (1988) Child Perpetrators – Children who Molest other Children. Child *Abuse and Neglect* 12: 219–29.

Johnson, T.C. and Doonan, R. (2005) Children with Sexual Behaviour Problems: What Have We Learned in the Last Two Decades? In M.C. Calder (ed.) *Children and Young People Who Sexually Abuse – New Theory, Research and Practice Developments* Lyme Regis: Russell House Publishers Ltd.

Jordon, J.V., Kaplan, A.G., Miller, J.B., Stiver, I.P. and Surrey, J.L. (1991) *Women's Growth in Connection: Writings from the Stone Centre* New York and London: The Guilford Press.

Kuhn, T. (1970) *The Structure of Scientific Revolutions* Chicago: Chicago University Press.

Labov, W. and Fanshell, D. (1977) *Therapeutic Discourse: Psychotherapy as Conversation* New York, San Francisco and London: Academic Press.

Lenderyou, G. and Ray, C. (eds) (1997) *Let's Hear it for the Boys* Sex Education Forum, National Children's Bureau.

Lew, M. (1990) *Victims No Longer: Men Recovering from Incest and Other Sexual Child Abuse* New York: Harper & Row Publishers.

MacLeod, M. and Saraga, E. (1988) Challenging the Orthodoxy: Towards a Feminist Theory and Practice. *Feminist Review* 28: 16–55.

McNamee, S. (1993) Research as Conversation. Conference paper: Constructed Realities: Therapy, Theory and Research, Norway.

McNamee, S. and Gergen, K.J. (eds) (1992) *Therapy as Social Construction* London: Sage.

Manning, P.K. and Cullum-Swan, B. (1994) Narrative, Content and Semiotic Analysis. In N. Denzin and Y. Lincoln (eds) *Handbook of Qualitative Research* London: Sage.

Mishler, E.G. (1986) *Research Interviewing: Context and Narrative* Cambridge, MA and London: Harvard University Press.

Mishler, E.G. (1990) Validation in Inquiry-guided Research: The Role of Exemplars in Narrative Studies. *Harvard Educational Review* 60: 415–42.

Mishler, E.G. (1991) Representing Discourse: The Rhetoric of Transcription. *Journal of Narrative and Life History* 1: 255–80.

Mishler, E.G. (1994) Narrative Accounts in Clinical and Research Interviews. (NB: All citations/quotations from personally provided pre-publication text of the paper, September 1994.) Now published in: B-L. Gunnarson *et al.* (eds) (1997) *The Construction of Professional Discourse* London: Longman.

Mishler, E.G. (1995) Models of Narrative Analysis: A Typology. *Journal of Narrative and Life History* 5: 87–123.

Mishler, E.G. (1996) Missing Persons: Recovering Developmental Stories/Histories. In R. Jessor, A. Colby and R.A. Shweder (eds) *Ethnography and Human Development: Context and Meaning in Social Enquiry* Chicago and London: University of Chicago Press.

Mishler, E.G. (2005) Commentaries on Potter and Hepburn, 'Qualitative Interviews in Psychology: Problems and Possibities', Commentary 3. *Qualitative Research in Psychology* 2: 315–18.

Mishler, E.G. (2006) Narrative and Identity: The Double Arrow of Time. In A. De Fina, D. Schiffrin and M. Bamberg (eds) *Discourse and Identity* Cambridge: Cambridge University Press.

Morrison, T. and Print, B. (1995) *Adolescent Sexual Abusers: An Overview* UK: NOTA.

Murray, M. (2003) Narrative Psychology. In J. Smith (ed.) *Qualitative Psychology* London: Sage.

Opie, A. (1992) Qualitative Research, Appropriation of the 'Other' and Empowerment. *Feminist Review* 40: 52–69.

Parker, I. (1992) Discourse Discourse: Social Psychology and Postmodernity. In J. Doherty, E. Graham and M. Malek (eds) *Postmodernism and Social Sciences* London: Macmillan.

Parker, I. (2005) Lacanian Discourse Analysis in Psychology: Seven Theoretical Elements. *Theory and Psychology* 15: 163–82.

Parton, N. and O'Byrne, P. (2000) *Constructive Social Work: Towards a New Practice* Hampshire and London: Macmillan Press Ltd.

Postlethwaite, J. (1998) A Critical Approach to Working with Young Abusers. *NotaNews* 28 December: 30–8.

Potter, J. and Hepburn, A. (2005) Qualitative Interviews in Psychology: Problems and Possibilities. *Qualitative Research in Psychology* 2: 281–307.

Potter, J. and Wetherell, M. (1987) *Discourse and Social Psychology* London: Sage.

Reinharz, S. (1992) *Feminist Methods in Social Research* New York and Oxford: Oxford University Press.

Riessman, C.K. (1993) *Narrative Analysis* London: Sage.

Riessman, C.K. (ed.) (1994) *Qualitative Studies in Social Work Research* Thousand Oaks and London: Sage.

Riessman, C.K. (2008) *Narrative Methods in the Human Sciences* London: Sage.

Riessman, C.K. and Quinney, L. (2005) Narrative in Social Work: A Critical Review. *Qualitative Social Work* 4(4): 391–412.

Robinson, S.L. (2005) Considerations for the Assessment of Female Sexually Abusive Youth. In M.C. Calder (ed.) *Children and Young People Who Sexually Abuse – New Theory, Research and Practice Developments* Lyme Regis: Russell House Publishers Ltd.

Rose, H. and Rose, S. (2001) *Alas Poor Darwin: Escaping Evolutionary Psychology* London: Vintage.

Rose, N. (1999) *Governing the Soul – the Shaping of the Private Self* London: Free Association Books.

Ryan, G. and Lane, S. (eds) (1997) *Juvenile Sexual Offending* (new and revised edition) San Francisco: Jossey-Bass Publishers.

Saleebey, D. (1994) Culture, Theory, and Narrative: The Intersection of Meaning and Practice. *Social Work* 39: 351–9.

Saleebey, D. (ed.) (1997) *The Strengths Perspective in Social Work Practice* New York: Longman.

Scott, J. and Telford, P. (2006) Similarities and Differences in Working with Girls and Boys Who Display Sexually Harmful Behaviour: The Journey Continues. In M. Erooga and H. Masson (eds) *Children and Young People Who Sexually Abuse Others – Current Developments and Practice Responses* (2nd edn) London and New York: Routledge.

Seidler, V.J. (1994) *Unreasonable Men: Masculinity and Social Theory* London and New York: Routledge.

Skuse, D., Bentovim, A., Hodges, J., Stevenson, J., Andreou, C., Lanyad, M., New, M., Williams, D. and McMillan, D. (1998) Risk Factors for Development of Sexually Abusive Behaviour in Sexually Victimised Adolescent Boys. *British Medical Journal* 317: 175–9.

Smith, J.A. (ed.) (2003) *Qualitative Psychology* London: Sage.

Stivers, C. (1993) Reflections on the Role of Personal Narrative in Social Science. *SIGNS: Journal of Women in Culture and Society* 18: 408–25.

Watkins, B. and Bentovim, A. (1992) The Sexual Abuse of Male Children and Adolescents: A Review of Current Research. *Journal of Child Psychology and Psychiatry and Allied Disciplines* 33: 197–248.

Wetherell, M. (1998) Positioning and Interpretative Repertoires: Conversation Analysis and Post-structuralism in Dialogue. *Discourse and Society* 9: 387–412.

Wetherell, M. (2003) Paranoia, Ambivalence, and Discursive Practices: Concepts of Position and Positioning in Psychoanalysis and Discursive Psychology. In R. Harre and F. Moghaddam (eds) *The Self and Others: Positioning Individuals and Groups in Personal, Political, and Cultural Contexts* Westport, CT and London: Praeger.

Wetherell, M. (2005) Unconscious Conflict or Everyday Accountability? *British Journal of Social Psychology* 44: 169–73.

Wetherell, M. (2008) Subjectivity or Psychodiscursive Practices? Investigating Complex Intersectional Identities. *Subjectivity* 22: 73–81.

Wetherell, M. and Edley, N. (1998) Gender Practices: Steps in the Analysis of Men and Masculinities. In K. Henwood *et al.* (eds) *Standpoints and Differences* London: Sage.

Wetherell, M. and Potter, J. (1992) *Mapping the Language of Racism: Discourse and the Legitimation of Exploitation* London: Harvester Wheatsheaf.

Wetherell, M. and White, S. (1990) 'Fear of Fat: Young Women Talking about Eating, Dieting and Body Image'. Unpublished Manuscript Text of talk at Bath University, Milton Keynes: Open University.

White, M. and Epston, D. (1990) *Narrative Means to Therapeutic Ends* New York: Norton.

Widdicombe, S. (1995) Identity, Politics and Talk: A Case for the Mundane and the Everyday. In S. Wilkinson and C. Kitzinger (eds) *Feminism and Discourse: Psychological Perspectives* London: Sage Publications.

Wilkinson, S. and Kitzinger, C. (eds) (1995) *Feminism and Discourse: Psychological Perspectives* London: Sage.

Williams, B. and New, M. (1996) Developmental Perspective on Adolescent Boys who Sexually Abuse other Children. *Child Psychology and PsychiatryReview* 1: 122–9.

Willig (2001) *Introducing Qualitative Research in Psychology* Buckingham: Open University Press.

Willig (2003) Discourse Analysis. In J. Smith (ed.) *Qualitative Psychology* London: Sage.

Index